No Voice
From The Hall

By the same author

NO VOICE
FROM THE HALL

*Early Memories of a
Country House
Snooper*

JOHN HARRIS

JOHN MURRAY
Albemarle Street, London

For Chrissy of Clifton Hampden

© John Harris 1998

First published in 1998
by John Murray (Publishers) Ltd,
50 Albemarle Street, London W1X 4BD

Reprinted 1998 (twice)

The moral right of the author has been asserted

A catalogue record for this book is available from the British Library

ISBN 0-7195-5567-1

Typeset in 11½/14½pt Bembo by Wearset, Boldon, Tyne and Wear.
Printed and bound in Great Britain by The University Press, Cambridge.

Contents

Contents

Contents

Illustrations

Illustrations

The author would like to thank the following for permission to reproduce photographs: Bruce Bailey, 21–22: Buckinghamshire County Council, 5: Sir Howard Colvin, 25, 77, 78, 81: Hillingdon Borough Libraries, 8, 18: K. Lomas, 54: National Monuments Record (RCHM England), 1–4, 6–9, 14–17, 19, 20, 23, 24, 26–30, 32–40, 43–46, 49, 55–61, 63, 66–71: Potters Bar Local History Society, 62: M.H. Ridgway, 74: Derek Sherborn, 44: Mrs Edmund Staunton, 82: Stockholm, Museum of Far Eastern Antiquities, 11: Waddesden Estate Office, 31. The following photographs are by the author: 12, 13, 47, 48, 50–53, 64, 65, 72, 73, 75, 76, 79, 80.

How it all began

THIS IS A tale of abandoned country houses, but also a personal odyssey of my experiences as an aspiring architectural historian, fishing and youth-hostelling my way around England after 1946. In my nomadic travels I discovered a situation that had no parallel elsewhere in Europe: a country of deserted country houses, many *in extremis*, most in a surreal limbo awaiting their fate. They suffered from vandalism, smelt of decay and dry rot, exuded a sense of hopelessness. The implements of execution were not the sword or the rope, but the sledgehammer, pick-axe and ball-and-chain, and frequently explosives. The situation was unique, because no other country had effected total mobilisation during the war, and certainly not Germany. It is extraordinary to realise that, away from the flow of armies between Russia and Normandy, the war might not have existed for many châteaux and schlosses. In Britain it was different, and the difference can be seen as a by-product of the 'Dunkirk spirit', for after Dunkirk nearly every country house had some role to play in the war effort, either through compulsory requisition or as a result of its owner offering it for patriotic uses. The story of what happened to a thousand of these houses is a horrific one that could be only partially told in the 'Destruction of the Country House' exhibition held at the Victoria and Albert Museum in 1974. The devastation wrought can be likened only to that inflicted by war.

What happened following 1945 was a continuum of two earlier crises that affected both the country house as a physical entity, and its way of life. The first serious threat to this world of landed interest was the great agricultural depression from the 1870s onwards. Because most landowners existed in a state of indebtedness and the income from agricultural rents was now insufficient to pay the interest, the Settled Land Law of 1882 had to be introduced to enable the sale of entailed heirlooms to meet mounting debts. In Britain as nowhere else, the floodgates were now opened for the disposal of works of art and valuable chattels on a scale hitherto regarded as inconceivable: collector moguls in the United States were the beneficiaries. One of the problems faced by the landed interest was the possession, often, of not one but several estates, each with a house. As debts mounted because rents were not coming in, so did the effects of recession: unwanted estates put up for sale and the house demolished; or, as a temporary measure, the sale of 'outlying parts'. Obviously, the crisis was always a personal one and varied from family to family. The munificently wealthy Duke of Sutherland was forced to demolish Sir Charles Barry's Trentham in Staffordshire in 1911, not because he could not afford it, but because of the stinking steam of pollution which rose from his lake. Giacomo Leoni's Palladian Bold Hall in Lancashire came down in 1900 because coal mining had isolated it. Even if there had been any awareness that a valuable heritage was being destroyed, there were few means of rescue: no amenity societies concerned with the problem, no National Trust, no state grants, no developed tourism – and apart from schools, private mental homes and some local authority adaptations, there were few alternative uses. We can sense the prevailing despair.

The second crisis followed the Armistice in 1918. During that war death duties were imposed and the families of those who had died for their country felt their effect most keenly: it was not uncommon for the head of the family, his elder son, and even that son's brother, all to have died on some foreign field. Despairing trustees simply could not cope with the multiple death duties – and so the houses came down. In the case of the approximately three to four hundred major losses between 1919 and 1939, the decision to demolish or sell differed from family to family. Some gave up easily. Others preferred to sell land and watch their estates – and their agricultural income – shrink. Selling chattels was an easy but only temporary solution. There are those who will say this way of life had to change, irrespective of wars and depressions, but that does not alter the fact that the loss to British architecture was probably as great as that from the destructions following the Dissolution of the Monasteries.

Before the 'Destruction of the Country House' exhibition there was a blurred understanding of the distinction to be made in the plight of country houses given over for patriotic use in the First World War and the Second. In the First War there was no compulsory requisition. Maybe a hundred owners offered their houses for use as hospitals or convalescent homes, and possibly many more were offered for other or partial use. Of these we have no information at all. In the next war the situation was different. Even before September 1939 some owners, in anticipation of the declaration of war, had already negotiated contracts for accommodating schools or evacuees moving out of endangered urban areas. So it was with Blenheim, Chatsworth and Longleat. They were the lucky ones. The belief that aerial bombing would instantly flatten cities had a galvanising effect, and as an emergency measure some organisations acquired country houses, like the Southern Railway Company, who bought Thomas Hope's Deepdene in 1939; in fact, their tenure of Deepdene extended until its demolition in 1969. Requisition increased once war was declared but, like the population, houses also enjoyed a 'phoney war'. There was little awareness on the part of government of just how many houses would be needed in the case of total mobilisation. Dunkirk changed all that, and by 1945 nearly every country house of any considerable size had been requisitioned by compulsory order. The exact number has never been ascertained, but must have approached two thousand at least. Only in a few circumstances did large houses escape requisition: such a case was Erddig, which accommodated a school for a while, until without light and with a failing water supply it was deemed uninhabitable.

Today it is difficult to comprehend the country house scene after 1940, especially in southern England in the year leading up to D-Day in 1944. The whole physical structure of the country was in a state of mobilisation. Nissen-hutted or prefabricated camps sprung up in parks, cheek by jowl with the great houses. Gardens and landscapes were violated by assault courses and mortar ranges, or embellished with lorries and tanks. Barbed wire fortified old fences. Sentry-boxes sprung up at park entrances. Rooms echoed to alien languages, as at Deene Park in Northamptonshire where Polish, Czech and

Indian regiments slept in Lord Cardigan's ballroom. The iron bedstead was ubiquitous. The treatment of requisitioned houses varied: Wilton, as HQ Southern Command, got off lightly, but lesser houses often suffered a lack of maintenance and custodial respect. If a down-pipe became clogged, it might remain like that for four years. The traveller·through England after 1945 journeyed in a dream-like landscape, so many empty mansions standing forlornly in their parks, all in a vacuum, awaiting the return of their owners to decide their ultimate fate; the process towards compensation was so slow that several houses collapsed in the interim. This state of uncertainty existed until well beyond 1960. One fact portrays the situation as no other: in 1955, one house was demolished every two and a half days.

Rolls Park in Essex is a typical case study of repatriated ownership. The Harveys (of circulation of the blood fame) owned Rolls from the seventeenth century, but in 1939 it passed to the impoverished Lloyd family, the father a humble parson. It was mostly seventeenth-century and Georgian, with a great carved Restoration staircase and a saloon reckoned one of the most beautiful rooms in England, plus what was virtually a family portrait gallery, each portrait enclosed in a rococo plaster frame. In 1939 Rolls was requisitioned for the army. The son, Andrew Lloyd, was called up and posted overseas. When he returned in 1945 he discovered that eighteen different regiments had occupied the house; they had 'hacked up the delectable back Tudor staircase' for firewood, and had begun on 'the Grinling Gibbons front staircase'. In the saloon, Allan Ramsay's famous portrait of Emma Harvey had been used as a dart-board, and she had been endowed with a moustache. On the periphery of north-east London, Rolls was surrounded by anti-aircraft guns of the largest calibre, which shook the house every night. Bombs fell nearby, and a V1 cleared the garden wall by inches and exploded, bringing off part of the roof. The conservative estimate given to Lloyd for repairs was £50,000, a huge sum then: the government offered £8,000. As he wrote to me, 'I threw in my hand in 1953 and allowed the house to be demolished. It was all too much.' This was the situation I encountered during my peregrinations across England after 1946.

I ought to explain how I came to make these travels. I was born to parents who could not cope with me – I even sometimes thought I was not theirs. It was sad that their view of me only changed when it was too late. I found refuge with my bachelor 'Uncle Sid', an endearing and intelligent man whom I affectionately called Snozzle because of his huge red bulbous nose. He went through the whole of the First World War in the Middlesex Regiment, had been seriously wounded, and stayed in France to work as a gardener on the staff of the Imperial War Graves Commission; he had returned to England, to a small bungalow in West Worthing, to be a shepherd on the South Downs. This was reflected in his sturdy frame made for walking. He was a good man possessed of a childlike innocence. He would lean upon a fence and talk to animals in a low voice. Cows stared at him transfixed. He was learned in the writings of Richard Jefferies (who had lived nearby), could recite chunks of him at will, and like that naturalist was a pantheist who would lie on the grass sward of ancient earthworks or tumuli, listening to voices from the earth. He was an enthusiastic member of the Society of Sussex Downsmen, and few were as familiar with the remote ways of the Downs as he. I followed in his footsteps. By the 1930s he had returned to his original work as an upholsterer and shared a workshop with his father in Uxbridge, but always moving back and forth to Worthing. There I more or less lived with him from 1946, when I was fifteen years old.

Sid had clearly inherited some gene from an earlier era. In the course of a St Paul's Girls' School project my daughter discovered that my family line on my father's side could be taken back to Henley, around 1810, where it disappears. It is our supposition, because of my extraordinary facial resemblance to the family of Harris, Earls of Malmsbury, who lived at Park Place, Henley at the time, that our family may have resulted from the coition of one of them with a local milkmaid. Sid certainly had unusual interests, and a taste for pictures and objects which he picked up from the many country house auctions he attended. He was the favoured upholsterer of west Middlesex and south Buckinghamshire, and worked in nearly all the country houses around. I was once the proud owner of an Astrakhan overcoat given Sid by the Duke of Kent in 1937 when he was upholstering at Coppins, the Kents' house near Iver.

I must also touch on fishing. Sid was an angler of distinction, with a 27-pound pike to his credit, and many exceptional roach and perch. He even fished the Somme, in 1915. I became a fisherman too. We would leave the house in the semi-darkness of dawn and before six o'clock, as day began to glimmer, we would be hunkered down by some reedy bank with the mist rising from the water. Our strategy in making piscatorial decisions was always to study our large-scale maps, following the blue line of watercourses. By this means we found many a virgin water, and this was my cartographical education, giving me the ability to read maps creatively. In Rowley lake near Langley Park, Buckinghamshire, we must have pulled out twenty fat roach of over a pound each in the first day we fished there. Fishing encouraged contemplation, and provided an excuse to explore houses and parks.

Fishing, country houses and the auctions of their contents came together for me in 1946, when Sid took me to my first country house sales. These spurred me on to see more houses that had been de-requisitioned, emptied of their contents, or faced an uncertain future.

One of the first sales Sid took me to was at Langley Park, which I had known since the age of eight, when I accompanied him there on an upholstery job. From my notes I see that our proximity to the demolished seat of the Tower family at Huntsmoor Park in Iver also prompted Sid to take me to view Captain C.T. Tower's seven-day sale at Weald Hall in Essex in July 1946, following the break-up of that great estate. I only remember a certain effulgence of the richest English furnishings associated with names such as Adam, Hepplewhite, Sheraton and Chippendale. As I refresh my memory with the catalogue, my eye lights upon two splendid oil sketches for painted stair-cases, by Sir James Thornhill. These were unknown to Edward Croft-Murray, author of the authoritative *Decorative Painting in England, 1537–1837* (1962). Now they tantalise me: I yearn to know for whom they were painted. Sid and I had long fished the Frays and the Colne through Huntsmoor Park, where the dace were particularly fine; and the nearby Colne Brook behind Delaford and Bridgefoot, where Martin Secker would allow us to go after trout, and I discovered Richings Park *in extremis* while fishing its long canal for tench. We both bicycled far and wide with our rods tied to our cross-bars, so I had fished the formal long canal at Bulstrode Park near Gerrards Cross long before I studied that house as a historian, and it was the same with abandoned Shardeloes, Stoke Park, Stoke Place, and Chalfont Park, with their fishy lakes.

Compulsory education ceased for me in June 1945, a couple of months before my fourteenth birthday. On that auspicious day of final release from tedious school my parents announced with trembling pride my apprenticeship in the upholstery workshop at Heal's, in Tottenham Court Road. Of course, I was never consulted. I need not dwell on my bitterness, only note that I was soon sacked, for extending my lunch break by several hours to work as an unpaid volunteer in the Prehistoric Department of the British Museum, sorting large cardboard boxes full of flint implements of every nationality. They had been stored and exhibited in the part of the museum blown up during the war, but thousands had been saved from the rubble. This sparked off a fleeting desire to become a prehistoric archaeologist. I then briefly worked for Astor, Boissilier and Lawrence in their laboratory at West Drayton near Cowley for testing waxes for X-rays. This was a ploy to obtain leave for further education at Acton Technical College, but naturally I never attended, skiving off instead to look for Acheulean flint axes in the gravel pits around West Drayton. Not surprisingly, I was copped, and released from my service to science. There were mutterings in the parental home, so I took refuge with Sid. I was now confronted by the dilemma of what to do next.

The government came to my rescue with the dole. Every Friday morning at the dole office in Uxbridge I received thirty shillings and sixpence. Then I took off, usually along the Oxford Road, hitch-hiking to who knows where, staying in youth hostels. I still have by me that lode-star of hostellers, the YHA *Handbook*. Mine is dated 1950, its black and mauve cover designed by Bernard B. West in a chiaroscuro wood-block style with village and church scene, boy and girl with bicycles, and boy with a rucksack. A night's stay cost one shilling and sixpence, breakfast was the same, and supper was

9

generally one shilling and ninepence. Provided I did odd jobs for wardens to earn a dinner or perhaps an extra night, that paltry gift from the State enabled me to tour for seven nights, returning to Uxbridge for the next week's tranche. Hostellers carried a card which would be stamped at each hostel; different-coloured inks were used, and each hostel boasted a different rubber stamp. There was competition to possess the most colourful card: it was a little like stamp-collecting. As a latter-day John Aubrey, William Stukeley or Celia Fiennes, I was awarded a year's subscription for the record number of youth-hostel stays in one year. However, the YHA *Handbook* did not always ensure accommodation. Twice I had the stars for company and once, frustrated in my attempts to get a lift, slept in the church of Maiden Bradley in Wiltshire, collecting the hassocks together for extra comfort. As I criss-crossed England I took in many of those two thousand country houses, empty, derelict or *in extremis*, and after a while I began to search them out.

Hitch-hiking meant that I was in the hands of kindly motorists (it was so very different then – no motorway madness, or aberrations of other sorts). From Denham I might not progress much further than Aylesbury – or I might, to my delight, be given a lift to Barnstaple. Once I was carried all the way to Lancashire and, by the sheer chance of the driver being a local farmer, saw the spectacular ruin of the abandoned Jacobean Kenyon Peel Hall, perhaps our greatest loss of any black-and-white half-timbered house, a casualty in 1955 through neglect and mining subsidence. Attempting to walk through the house meant climbing up sloping floors. On another occasion I enjoyed an equally long lift, from Thame to Castleford in Yorkshire. Little did I know I had landed in the middle of a mining area that was the cause of a country-house blitz in the locality: Parlington Hall, Byram Hall, Pontefract Park – now all gone. Another lift, towards Garforth on the way to the Dacre Banks hostel near Harrogate, brought me and the driver literally up sharp, at the astonishing view across the park of the gutted shell of Kippax Park, a Gothick extravaganza designed by Daniel Garrett in the 1750s. So long was its façade that it seemed to take up the whole horizon. It had truly been gutted, I think for a very long time. On another hitch (and I can pin-point it accurately to December 1948), I was returning from either the Heasley Mill or the Parracombe hostel in North Devon and serendipitously obtained a lift in South Molton from an antique dealer going to the Halswell Park auction where Lord Wharton was selling the Kemeys-Tynte family portraits. Only vaguely do I remember the park with its many ornamental follies – all intact then. Years later I returned to Somerset with my wife Eileen and Hermione Hobhouse, in pursuit of Halswell's seventeenth-century architect, William Taylor, and Thomas Wright the Wizard of Durham, Georgian astronomer, architect and garden designer. In the course of this dole-induced activity I also spent many weekends with Sid on the South Downs, where one amble took us to the remote and decayed hunting park of Tudor Michel Grove, and we found that its early eighteenth-century Dutch pavilion was still standing. We continued on across the downs to Slindon House, and the mysterious discovery of cupboards of valuable porcelain.

All points of the compass were mine to choose from. Until recently I still had my torn and rubbed *Geographia* map of England, kept as a relic (I had not then graduated to the one-inch Ordnance Survey maps for long journeys). As well as the whims of motorists, favourite youth hostels determined my itinerary: Astwell Castle in Northamptonshire, a fragment of

George Shirley's great house of 1606; the thirteenth-century St Briavels Castle in Gloucestershire; the Elizabethan Wilderhope Manor in Shropshire; Jacobean Harrowby Hall in Lincolnshire; and Littledown Farm near Milton Abbas in Dorset. Twice I stayed at the Welsh Bicknor hostel, delighting in the great fortress of Goodrich Castle but failing to get into Edward Blore's Goodrich Court, firmly shut up and waiting for demolition: how I later regretted this. At the time, I understood from the caretaker that the house had already been numbered in parts for shipment to California for some film star. It was on a foray from Welsh Bicknor that I found the magical Aramstone, standing desolate in the enclosure of an old mill, stables and offices. In retrospect, it was perhaps here more than anywhere else that I first sensed the crisis of post-war destruction. Aramstone dated from about 1730, late Baroque in style, and the interiors remained as they were first built. As I clambered through an open window and walked the deserted rooms, I shared the anguish of the house. I caressed the walnut stair balustrade, unable to believe that this precious example of Georgian craftsmanship would soon be chopped up or burnt (although frequently the upright balusters of staircases were torn out and sold off). Almost every room had pretty later neo-classical chimney-pieces, of coloured marbles inserted in 1730s pilastered frames. Fortunately I had left the house the way I came in before a ferocious farmer booted me out of the grounds. The owners, described in an official report as 'hunting people who live in Cornwall', wanted to pull it down – and that was that. As at picturesque Bayons Manor in Lincolnshire, a nasty bungalow is its memorial. The second time I stayed at Welsh Bicknor I came across nearby Harewood Park in Herefordshire, standing empty by its tiny Victorian church. I remember fronts of about 1700, much altered inside in the later Georgian period for Sir Henry Hoskyns, empty rooms, the doors and windows open. In fact, Harewood was not *in extremis*, simply and sadly unwanted. It came down in 1952, like Willoughby Hall in Lincolnshire, blown up by the local militia.

I'm not sure whether it was on this Herefordshire circuit or on one from Wilderhope that I sheltered from thunder and lightning in Wisteston Court. My topographical bible in those days was, as indeed it still is, Murray's *Hand Book* to each county. I had read, under 'Marden', of the church built by Offa over Saint Ethelbert's interment and of the miraculous spring, Ethelbert's well. As I was walking along without a lift on a deserted road it started to pour with rain, and I found derelict Wisteston. I can't believe it is still there, but I hope so. The house creaked with decay, the ruined library was a cynosure of despair, the upstairs rooms flapping with birds, their droppings inches thick on the floor. On another occasion I had been given a lift by the warden from Wilderhope to Wellington. On the next lift, *en route* to the Abbey Foregate hostel in Shrewsbury, I spied an enticing empty house a mile or so out of Wellington, got out, and found Apley Castle, of the 1790s and 1850s, another loss in that terrible year of 1955. It was not a house of great merit, but retained an elegantly disposed staircase hall and a few Greekly-ordered rooms. What struck me was that nearly all the ornamental detail had been smashed or torn off by vandals, and every window broken.

Perhaps I should attempt to describe the sensual and emotional effect of discovering a house *in extremis*. Estate care has been abandoned within the park perimeter, the hedgerows are unkempt. A clear divide is discernible at the gate or lodge between the public road and the drive across the park: on one side maintenance, on the other decay. The lodge might be shut up, the gates locked. The drive is crumbling, often weeded over. A decayed park in late spring or summer, the parkland ungrazed, colourful with wild flowers, the lawns unmown and garden divisions returned to nature: so many of my houses appear to me in this floral frame. There is always a certain apprehension in the walk between lodge and house, not knowing what to expect. The eye is vigilant and there is caution in the approach, watch kept for signs of opposition. Once the house is in view it is advisable to look casual, not furtive. Watch for broken windows, scattering of rubbish: both are good signs for the country-house prowler. At this juncture the house always seems to be cocooned in a pressing silence. There is a blankness in its glassy stare.

Between 1946 and 1960 I must have visited more than two hundred houses. If the house was already gone, I would be emotionally affected by the staring sore gap of the site of its foundations. Crumbling balustraded terraces protecting nothing and overlooking a park turned to arable, or garden trees framing a void, only accentuated the tragedy of loss. Panshanger in Hertfordshire was demolished in 1954. Beyond the Tudoresque lodge on the public road the untended drive passes through overgrown shrubberies, with here and there broken Gothick garden ornaments, to debouch upon the plateau where the house once stood. This offers two prospects: one of a sublime Reptonian landscape dropping away to the river Mimram, the other, upon the plateau itself, the empty untenanted site of the house, of bumpy grass over the brick and masonry foundations. On one side a barbed-wire fence hints of something special to be protected – nothing less than the spectral ruin of one of the grandest greenhouses in England, once standing all in its glory with William Atkinson's

Gothic house built for the 5th Earl Cowper from 1807 to 1820. When I stood in the greenhouse I was reminded of Woodfold Hall in Lancashire, derelict since 1956, its beautiful Ionic neo-classical greenhouse entirely taken over by nature with trees growing up through it, stone columns cheek by jowl with tree trunks. At Teddesley Park in Staffordshire, demolished in 1954, I found on its grassy plateau just two grand baroque brick stable ranges with strong rusticated stone windows. They surveyed the landscape with no purpose, the formal outlines of the garden long since erased. Or there can remain just nothing, as I discovered when searching frantically for evidence of that great Midlands house, Gopsall Park in Leicestershire, its suites of rooms once a triumph of English rococo taste, all destroyed in 1951. It might never have existed. Every sign, even the lodge, had been scraped away, I believe by the Crown Estates. Nothing is more emotive than to visit the site of Wanstead House on the north-east edge of London, where a hole in the ground marks the cellars of what was once the noblest Palladian house in England, its great formal gardens still there in ghostly outline. Such places are now the delight of the new breed of garden archaeologist.

The Milton Abbas hostel at Littledown Farm was my favourite. The warden was friendly, and cooked delicious casseroles: I stayed there half a dozen times. There was yoghurt from his goats, and he always offered an extra night for help. From Littledown I discovered Georgian Blandford, though it was only later that the architectural historian Howard Colvin introduced me to the 'Bastards of Blandford', the family of architect-builders who stamped their provincial Baroque style upon the town after the fire of 1731. As an uneducated youth ignorant of Norman Shaw I viewed Bryanston School circumspectly, but enjoyed my discovery of

Langton House. Walking along the river Stour I noticed a disused and inviting drive, which drew me to C.R. Cockerell's masterpiece, built for J.J. Farquharson in 1827. I sensed a Palladian style – not a bad judgement for a callow youth. The caretaker was hostile, but after palm-greasing persuasion she allowed me to see the dramatic staircase walled with coloured scagliola. What a terrible loss when it was demolished in 1949. I walked on to Tarrent Crawford, spying Spetisbury village across the river, unaware then of the baroque Spetisbury House, by one of the Bastards, demolished in 1927. I was reminded of my first visit to Blandford a few years ago, when Tim Knox, now Architectural Historian to the National Trust but then a deputy curator of the Drawings Collection of the Royal Institute of British Architects, acquired Cockerell's model for Langton House.

In 1949 National Service was hanging over me – not that I was worried or apprehensive, but I felt I was losing control of my destiny. Sid and I attended two major sales that year. In July it was the Duke of Manchester's at Kimbolton Castle in Huntingdonshire, with its dazzling display of Venetian ambassadorial treasures and of heirlooms, many belonging to Catherine of Aragon, where Sid bought me a royal crown she was said to have embroidered. I have since come to know Kimbolton well, and to relate its decorations by Giovanni Antonio Pellegrini to those at Narford Hall in Norfolk. In October Sid and I attended the auction at Campsey Ash in Suffolk where Viscount Ullswater was selling the Lowther and Lonsdale portraits. I wish I had known more about architectural and garden history then: few historians took note of its interiors, and its decayed gardens, then celebrated for their lead statuary and urns, all since dispersed, have been the subject of modern garden archaeology. Sid bought two small mahogany tea tables.

These were my last sales before the long hiatus in my life which was National Service.

December 1949 found me at Crookham Barracks near Fleet in Hampshire for six weeks of basic training, followed by four more pleasurable weeks at the Army School of Hygiene at Mychett. I must confess to a sneaking delight in the precision of 'square-bashing'. There were also several weekends at Farnham with its castle, tea shops and bookshops, a route march to Waverley Abbey in ignorance of Colen Campbell's villa there, an Army Education Corps visit to Farnborough Abbey, and the discovery of empty Dogmersfield Park. Then I was sent to Malaya, which meant other things and other experiences, including being stranded on Pulau Langkawi, then a desert island. After demobilisation in December 1951 I lived in Paris and spent some months as a student at the École du Louvre, which marked the beginning of a more European cultural education. I came back to Sid for the month of July 1952, which happily coincided with the sale of the contents of Fawley Court in Oxfordshire following Major MacKenzie's death, where Sid bought several lots of fabrics. The history of John Freeman of Fawley, Georgian antiquarian and amateur architect, passed me by, however.

After Paris I was on the dole again, which meant more encounters with houses in my peripatetic life, notably Badger Hall in Shropshire. Fishing was a temporary panacea for the uncertainties of life. More fishing at Denham Court led to the discovery on one piscatorial foray there of abandoned Breakspears House, near Harefield. Whenever I leave Heathrow now and look down as the plane climbs, I see old fishing grounds disfigured by the tentacles of airport service and access roads and the new Staines Reservoirs. Between West Drayton and Staines the Great Western Railway's branch line served fishermen at Poyle Halt and Yeoveney station. Here the river Colne and Colne Brook and the Wraysbury River flow towards the Thames. On our bicycles Sid and I used to pass the market gardens which were soon to become Heathrow. Surprisingly, the old parks are still there – Richings, Stanwell, Hanworth, Cranford – but now the airport perimeters are approaching them like an incoming tide. If you are in the right seat at the right time, the great park wall of Lord Boling-broke's Dawley, a mile in extent, can still be seen as your plane climbs out of Heathrow.

My short stint working for Nikolaus Pevsner on the editing of his *Buildings of England* series occurred in 1953. I had 'joined the club', or so I thought. Alas, I disagreed with much he did. I objected to his wasteful method of having information abstracted onto pieces of paper by two dear German émigrée ladies, who might just as well have been gathering information on golf courses, for all they knew about architecture. I objected to his neglect of design documentation: not once in his life did he ever venture into the RIBA Drawings Collec-tion. Even at that time I could not understand why he never took Howard Colvin into his confidence. I objected also to his disdain for more localised topographical literature, such as Keate's *Middlesex* or Dodsley's *London*. And as for Vicary Gibbs's thirteen volumes of the *Complete Peerage*, guide to all the owners of the houses he described, it might never have existed. It was with relief on both sides that I was given the boot after three months. Yet Pevsner *was* a spur, and *was* a mentor, and he knew I recognised him as such. He was then travelling the counties for his *Buildings of England* series, and I often followed in his footsteps. The key auction event of my Pevsner period was the tragic Ashburnham of Ashburnham sale in Sussex, in June and July 1953, a sale which has passed into legend. There I bought my set of Napoleonic Egyptian Revival plates, from a larger service. I have a dim memory of C.L. Clérisseau's painted panel decoration in the saloon, a stronger one of the rich and sumptuous Boulle furniture which had been bought by Lord Ashburnham from the Duc de Richelieu's sale in Paris in 1788. At the sale, although I did not know it, were the historian Rupert Gunnis and the antique dealer Geoffrey Houghton Brown, later to become two of my closest friends.

The *Buildings of England* initiated in me a new discipline, that of relating what I saw to documents and topographical accounts: the birth pains of an architectural historian had begun. The process was hastened when in 1954 Geoffrey Houghton Brown and Francis Collin employed me in their antique shop, Collin and Winslow, in the Fulham Road, with weekend superintendence of Geoffrey's Winslow Hall in Buckinghamshire. This was the fourth of his large country-house purchases: Waresley Park, Huntingdonshire in 1934; Culham House, Berkshire, in 1937; and Felix Hall, Essex, in 1938. This last housed Lord Western's Roman antiquities, and cost Geoffrey £1,750. He took off the later Georgian wings, so reducing it to its original early eighteenth-century villa form. War was declared, it was requisitioned by the army in 1940, and they effectively burnt it down in 1941. I visited the shell with Geoffrey in 1955. The walls stood vacant, but Western's Roman mosaic was still in the hall pavement. I think Geoffrey made a small flat in the basement, with the gutted shell and mosaic above.

With Collin and Winslow I was at a watershed. I recollect my first meeting with Geoffrey for tea at 20 Thurloe Square, where I was dazzled to be welcomed in a room caparisoned in colourful decorative works of art and furnishings. He looked, as he did at his death forty years on, most delicate in complexion, his hands long and beautiful, his deportment and dress most elegant. Even then I sensed his self-effacement. He was an *éminence grise* to so many, not least Felix Harbord, the brilliant decorator. Indeed Geoffrey had himself been a stylish and influential *moderne* decorator between 1927 and 1933, an achievement he hardly spoke of until he was 'discovered' in the 1980s. Geoffrey offered me the basement flat in 20 Thurloe Square for twenty-five shillings a week all thrown in, including Miss Hall the housekeeper and the left-overs from the substantial meals taken 'upstairs'. I had as company Alessandro Vittoria's bust of Doge Priuli, two chairs with the Chantilly inventory stamp, and a white marble neo-classical chimney-piece reputedly from Samuel Wyatt's Temple House in Berkshire, demolished in 1930. I found myself at the bottom of a house with Jim Lees-Milne at the top and Geoffrey and Ronald Fleming in between. What a delectable sandwich! After the Oratory service an eclectic group would gather there for Sunday lunch – there might be Father d'Arcy from Farm Street, the Ministry of Works architect Adrian Brookholding-Jones, the decorators John Fowler and Felix Harbord, Cecil Beaton, Gerald Berners, Ralph Dutton, the painter Roy de Maistre, or Delves Molesworth from the V&A. Ronald was a partner in the distinguished firm of decorators and antique dealers Mann and Fleming and had lived with Geoffrey since 1933. I thought him a dull stick, and found it difficult to associate him with the flair of his firm.

Geoffrey's buying forays and those of his friend Felix Harbord (familiarly known as 'Cardboard') provided me with opportunities to attend country-house auctions, usually in houses under threat. My notes catalogue a series of visits prompted by Geoffrey's enthusiasms: Badger, Belvedere, Bulstrode, Kempshott, The Grange, Onslow, Scrivelsby, Stratton, Warnford, Winchendon, and so many others. The first auction I went to under the tutelage of Collin and Winslow was the 'attic' sale held at Claydon House in Buckinghamshire, prior to its handover to the National Trust. How silly Ralph Verney was to sell so many attractive furnishings and objects: sets of Grand Tour cork models by Altieri and Chichi bought by the 2nd Lord Verney in Italy, dozens of family portraits of the Highmore or Hudson sort, masses of elaborate woodwork by the genius carver Mr Lightfoot, and a *bureau-plat* on which Geoffrey found the stamp of Cressent.

At this time too I met that sensitive Ministry of Works investigator, the kindly Derek Sherborn, always willing to 'invest' a country house at my suggestion. Derek, collector and *marchand amateur*, was the unsung pioneering investigator of the old Ministry of Housing and Local Government, and possessed a good eye. Fawns Manor at Bedfont in Middlesex was his showpiece. He reminds me that we 'invested' nearby Stanwell Place together and found the remains of the ornamental buildings by James Gibbs, its formal gardens by Charles Bridgeman, and the King of Iraq in the house. We discovered, in a suburban road near Weybridge, the baroque William Talman gate piers of Dorchester House, Surrey, with their trophies alluding to Lord Portmore's military exploits, long before I produced my *Talman*.

The signal event of 1954 was my correspondence, and subsequent meeting, with Howard Colvin and Rupert Gunnis. With sympathetic interest and encouragement they showed me that architectural history was a discipline to be mastered – but not in the way recommended by Pevsner: 'You will have to acquire a degree,' he said; 'No,' I replied, 'I'll get somewhere by my own volition' – and, most importantly, to be enjoyed. Hardly had I begun to correspond with Rupert than he commanded me to the delectable Hungershall Lodge, off the Common at Tunbridge Wells, where he lived. I learnt much from his libraries, and from his convivial and racy conversation. Many were the days or the weekends that we made a tour in Kent, or East Sussex. With him I paid a second visit to the ill-fated Belvedere at Erith, and with him drove over to see the smoking remains of the Cromwellian Syndale House, both in Kent. We saw Brightling Park, Sussex, with its glorious Palladian Great Room added in 1745. Rupert fulminated at the owners for its destruction in 1955.

One excursion provided me with a link back to my downland wanderings with Sid. Sometime before 1949 Sid and I had had a tempting view of John Nash's West Grinstead Park from the park walls (I have a vague memory that Sid was following in the footsteps of Michael Fairless, the author of that minor English classic, *The Roadmender*). With the patrician Rupert access was easy, and we could hardly believe the elegance of the Gothic rooms soon to be destroyed. The circular dining-room was filled with sacks of potatoes. Despite a feasible plan to reduce the house to two ranges, down it came in 1965. With Mr Pratley, of Hall's Bookshop, Tunbridge Wells and Rupert's executor, we drove to Hampshire in July 1955 to attend the break-up of the Sloane Stanleys' lovely Regency Paultons prior to its imminent demolition. Here Rupert bought me Prosser's *Hampshire*, which had found its way to Paultons from another endangered Hampshire house, Norman Court. Nearer home, we attended the Duchess of Wellington's sale at Penns in the Rocks in January 1957. I was recently reminded by Derek Sherborn that at Stratfield Saye in Hampshire I slipped on the wet terrace, bringing down with me clasped in my arms the lesbian Duchess, known as the 'Dyke Duchess'. That year Rupert also took me to the Countess of Derby's sale at Cowarth Park near Sunningdale. During this period both Rupert and Howard enjoined me to combine my passion for country houses with exploring the family papers in their muniment rooms and libraries, and publishing what I found. Howard's *Dictionary of English Architects, 1660–1840* had appeared in 1954, instantly endowing him with the title of our lexicographer of architectural history. His *Dictionary* revolutionised the writing of English architectural history. No one has been more generous in sharing information.

This was a determinant. Did I really want to be an antique dealer? My fate was sealed by having Jim Lees-Milne hovering above me in Thurloe Square, like a guardian angel. I had only been in the house two days when I boldly knocked on his door, and soon we were sitting on the sofa like a reunion of two old friends. Through his recommendation to Jimmy Palmes, the RIBA Librarian, I was invited to join the Library and Drawings Collection at a princely salary of £340 a year, £20 less than I was getting at Collin and Winslow. With regret, I decided to leave that agreeable commercial womb. I was never good at polishing furniture, and recollect Paul Wallraf, who came in one day to buy a bronze, fuming at my incompetent wrapping (nevertheless, I remained a welcome visitor to his glitzy treasure house in Grosvenor Gardens). At the RIBA the hunt for drawings took me to more houses. One speciality was to take drawings in the RIBA collection to the house they depicted – a sure entrance ticket and guarantee of lunch or tea. I had a great time following up all the William Burn and MacVicar Anderson designs.

I returned to Pevsner's fold when he recognised that I could write and in 1957 asked me to contribute articles to the *Archi-*

tectural Review. At a meeting a year later he confessed that the *Buildings of England* series was going to be so protracted that he might never finish it in his lifetime. 'Would you like to co-operate on a volume?' he asked. I enthusiastically agreed, and chose Lincolnshire because it was a largely undocumented county of which I already knew something: I had stayed in the Harrowby Hall youth hostel near Grantham, had discovered Willingham House and Bayons Manor with Sid, and Tattershall Castle and Scrivelsby Court with Geoffrey, discoveries which spurred me on to see more of this unknown rural county. Now at another watershed, I attended my last auction with Geoffrey at Cobham Hall in Kent on 22 July 1957, the 8th Earl of Darnley's sale. The Roman antiquities were mouth-watering. Geoffrey bought two marble cinerary urns, and I a splendid chimney bas-relief, attributed to Rysbrack but probably by Thomas Carter. I have it still.

Lincolnshire was now on the agenda. The index cards I riffle through, onto which I transcribed essential information and stuck my box Brownie snaps, bear witness to my morbid fascination with empty, derelict houses. One such was Thonock Hall, sitting gloomily outside Gainsborough, abandoned by the Hickman Bacons after 1947, eventually demolished in 1964. Many of the distinguished family pictures had been lent to Gainsborough Hall, a surprise and bonus for the unknowing visitor to that great ancient house. In 1959 I described Thonock as 'forlorn faced', and could not obtain access. When I did so later, I marvelled at the rich late-Regency decor, with eighteenth-century panelling incorporated from the earlier house.

Another discovery was Temple Belwood in the mysterious Isle of Axeholme, a ruin I should have given far more attention to than I did. With Scrivelsby in mind I noted that 'the

Early Georgian style does not make for suggestive ruins'. Temple Belwood had been reduced to the ground floor, the whole camouflaged with foliage and brambles. It was an open aviary, the birds rising out of the rooms with great flappings of wings, the collapsing timbers of a house beyond redemption crisscrossed, draped with the hairy plasterwork of ceilings that were no more. It was a return to nature. Temple Belwood was a large, plainly-detailed brick house, and I was certainly wrong about the date: a lead plaque recorded that William and Susanna Johnson had built the north front in 1787 (to the designs of a Samuel Foster, maybe from Doncaster). I did record Squire Johnson's fifty-foot obelisk in memory of his favourite dog and horse. Oh! the ruins and lost houses noted on my cards: Allington, Aswarby, Blankney, Bloxholm, Cockerington, Elkington, Easton, Gautby, Glentworth, Hagnaby, Haverholme, Langton, Manby, Northorpe, Riby, Scremby, Scrivelsby, Stainfield, Sudbrook, Syston and Walmsgate. Poor Walmsgate: a lovely stone house, most chastely detailed, and built in 1824 – I think, now, by C.H. Tatham, who worked in the locality, and not by Sir Robert Smirke, my first guess. There was also a free-standing Arts and Crafts chapel, built by Henry Wilson for Thomas Yorke Dallas Yorke in 1901, in memory of his son who died in the Boer War, completely decorated and kitted out. Now all is gone, although the chapel was reincarnated as St Hugh, Langworth, in 1960. The insensitive Forestry Commission just planted up to the very walls of the house, their trees marching across the ornamental Edwardian gardens.

Of all the abandoned houses I saw, especially in that wondrously hot and sultry summer of 1959, only *one* has survived – Horkstow Hall, the Georgian rebuilding of Sir Thomas Darrell's Jacobean house whose plan by the Elizabethan surveyor

John Thorpe has been preserved for us in a volume of drawings in Sir John Soane's Museum. A very strange tale attaches to Horkstow Hall, and it is not on my cards, nor of my telling. In 1959 the house stood empty and seemingly abandoned. Needing to get in, I discovered in a cottage nearby a surprisingly articulate farm worker in his eighties who had been at Horkstow since 1894. Taking me round, in a bedroom upstairs he remarked, 'There were horses painted here before the war' – meaning the First World War, and explaining how they had been exposed when wallpaper was taken off after a flood. He then referred to a tradition in the locality of a painter who had dissected horses hanging from iron hooks in the beams of a nearby barn. I mentioned the name of George Stubbs, but it meant nothing to the Horkstow ancient. Stubbs certainly had north Lincolnshire connections: in 1754 he was sent to Italy by Mrs Nelthorpe of Scawby, and in 1758 came to remote Horkstow to dissect specimens for his *Anatomy of the Horse*, which was published in 1766. Perhaps he lodged in the house. The tale deserves telling, because it has a ring of truth: oral evidence from one who could have been recollecting family or local lore only two long generations removed from the lifetime of Stubbs.

Visiting abandoned houses required strategy, and sometimes no small spice of deceit. For my Lincolnshire researches I carried with me a letter from Pevsner describing the purpose of my travels, and had informed the Lincoln constabulary. I recollect one amusing incident: approaching a house, I took one look, found it boring, turned around and left. As I did so, a face appeared at a window and a voice called. I took no notice, mounted my Lambretta and puttered off. A short while later I noticed that a policeman on a moped was following me at a discreet distance. I thought up a mischievous ruse. It was

time for lunch, so stopping at a church I went in, my sand-
wiches in a bag. Half an hour later I casually left, and the
policeman pounced: "Ere, yoo, what yer got in that bag?' or
words to that effect. Furious at finding no church plate, he
looked over my letter, reddened, and said, 'I believe yoo've
'ad me on, sir,' then wobbled away on his moped. Poor village
bobby. I felt a beast.

How many Lincolnshire houses have I walked through, up
and down, in and out, without finding a soul at home! I could
have cleared the lot in a pantechnicon. In those halcyon days,
security was of little concern. I remember entering Edenham
church and finding the Renaissance gold and silver plate given
to the Duke of Ancaster when he was Ambassador in Vienna,
just piled on the altar. Redbourne Hall was like the *Marie
Celeste*, but not so the nearby vicarage, where room after room
was filled with the vicar's paintings of naked boys. 'No sound
from the chamber, no voice from the hall' at Thorpe Tilney or
Grimblethorpe Hall, and at lovely Oxcombe, hidden in its
secret valley, I walked from top to bottom calling out, in case
the owner was asleep. I even snatched a glass of water in the
kitchen. So enamoured was I of this remote place that I
dreamed of marrying the châtelaine, if there were one.

In visiting country houses that were still lived in, the strategy differed with each situation. Grand houses demanded a
prior appointment, but if the house was only moderately grand
it might be enough to ask to look around the outside first,
then enquire, 'Could I see just the staircase?' – which might
lead to seeing everything, or being given the boot. It was
sometimes necessary to fib and invent tales, depending on the
tone of the first wary confrontation. If there was hostility it
was generally better to offer a sound explanation, rather than
the lame 'I'm interested in architecture'. I often found it useful

to be the descendant of a younger son of the family who in the mid nineteenth century had emigrated to Australia, South Africa, Kenya or Canada.

Another ploy was to pretend to own a painting or drawing of the house. This worked marvellously at Mavisbank, Midlothian, renowned for its abusive custodian who kept Dobermann pinschers and was all too ready to unleash them. With Marcus Binney, that champion of heritage issues and later (from 1975) President of SAVE Britain's Heritage, I circumspectly approached the mess of rusting cars and caravans littering the forecourt of this ravishingly beautiful Scottish villa. At the first nasty onslaught from the Dobermann fancier, I commented that my family owned a painting of the house; might I take a snap for confirmation? It worked.

Many's the time I've invented drawings held at the RIBA to gain access. I believe it is never wise to speak about the 'problem of endangered houses' for fear of prompting an answer like 'Don't want Ministry nosey-bodies round here'. Once, at Stubbers in Essex in 1958, confronted by a militant carer, I said my mother had been an under-maid in the house and wanted to know if the 'damned place' (a wonderful early eighteenth-century brick house) had been pulled down. The carer replied that demolition would soon take place, so I added that she had also said, 'And good riddance too.'

Another ploy was to pretend to be someone I was not. I've been Lord Bellasye or Humphrey Prideaux, looking at houses visited by an ancestor in 1832. But take care – the unexpected can happen, as it did in 1954 when the antique dealer and decorator David Vicary and I wanted to see that gaunt, gutted ruin of Sir Jeffry Wyatville's Rood Ashton in Wiltshire. 'Keep Out' and 'No Trespassing' notices encircled it. In the church we had seen the monument to its builders, Walter Long and his wife. As we negotiated a boundary fence, a man emerged out of a habited wing, sharply demanding an explanation. I countered with the assertion that my family on my mother's side were Longs, through my great-grandfather's wife in Australia. To my embarrassment he replied, 'Then we're related. I'm a Long too, but – ha! ha! – maybe, like you, a long way from the Longs who were here. It's only coincidence I'm here. Come in and have some tea.' Never did I realise how well I knew our old house in Sydney, called Long Rood. I spoke of prints of the house on the walls, and the legend that some of Wyatville's drawings had been in the family. I said I'd visited my relatives just once, but they now lived in Perth. I never did send Mr Sam Long the promised genealogy.

There was always the unexpected. I will not comment upon the naked lady who met me at the door of a Wolds farmhouse – or the consequences. I was enquiring for Stubbs's Barn. Rural places like the remoter parts of agrarian Lincolnshire seemed to retain certain of the primal passions found in characters from Hardy's novels. I found a love-in going on at Witham-on-the-Hill, and it was not uncommon, particularly with farmhouses, for faces to watch me from windows, never to reveal themselves further. Many empty houses sheltered tramps, especially the old-fashioned sort that called at doors to have their tin filled up with hot water and in hope of something more. I found a very amiable tramp living in Cothelstone House in Somerset, comfortably bedded down on a mattress, with a fire in the grate, in a room with pretty Pompeian decorations. Maybe he stayed there until the house went, in 1964.

At Fornham Hall in Suffolk, a James Wyatt house of 1785, an inviting open back door led to a suite of handsome neo-classical rooms, with Greekly ones decorated in 1824 by

Robert Abraham for the 12th Duke of Norfolk. I had just taken my first step on the stairs when I heard someone walking up and down; I paused to listen, and the walking continued; I paused longer, and still the pacing continued. It was too spooky, so I beat a retreat and watched from a distance. Yet no one emerged, no face came to the window of a house apparently abandoned. At Paxton Hall in Huntingdonshire, I had a much nastier experience. I had 'invested' the place after seeing what remained of Geoffrey's Waresley Park, and recollect looking up at a Georgian façade, then turning the corner to find very ugly Victorian extensions with a tower. Entering through a conservatory full of refuse and signs of wartime requisition, I was beginning to admire a spatially splendid stair when two spivvy thugs, clearly *not* caretakers, came hurtling down them. They breathed into my face, asked what I wanted, then took me by the arm and pushed me out, threatening 'Or else!' I cleared off pretty sharp.

Towards the end of 1959 I was living in David Vicary's flat in Eccleston Street, above Roy de Maistre in the sculptor Chantry's old studio, with Mrs Courtauld, shortly to become Rab Butler's second wife, in between. I was soon to be seconded to the Avery Library at Columbia University, which led to the discovery of my wife, and of rooms taken out of many of the very houses I had seen *in extremis*, which had been transported to America. Alas, the destruction did not abate, and 'so they all came down', as I wrote in 1974. After the terrible 1950s, the 1960s were not much better, and it was even worse in Scotland, where the National Trust had been ineffectual. The minutes of the Georgian Group tell all. How could we lose Chambers's Duntish Court in 1965, a perfect entity inside and out? It was a survival of the best of his early decoration, comparable to Lord Bessborough's Roehampton House.

Sad to say, when I found this empty house I had not yet come to a full appreciation of Chambers's worth. It was a loss as bad as that of Wilton Park near Beaconsfield, Buckinghamshire. Richard Jupp had designed the house for Josiah Dupré, Governor of Madras, in about 1790. C.H. Tatham added wings in 1803 and provided elegant neo-Grecian interiors. It had survived as built and was then the officers' mess of the Royal Army Education Corps. I marvelled at its perfection. Yet when in 1967 it was replaced by a mediocre Property Services Agency tower block, no one complained, and the Georgian Group was compliant.

'The Destruction of the Country House' exhibition in 1974 was a turning-point, not only for its theatrical revelation of the terrifying scale of a loss such as had never been sustained by any country in any period, except as a result of war, but because it offered alternatives to despair and destruction. It showed institutions and offices the advantages of locating in country houses outside urban centres. It displayed the growing mettle of the Historic Buildings Council in making grants to owners on condition of reasonable public access, and the success of the National Trust in acquiring endangered properties. It showed the attraction of converting houses into flats and apartments, by Mutual Households for the retired or by the entrepreneurial Kit Martin for anyone who wanted to live in a historic house. Not least, the 'Destruction' exhibition, though it did not offer a panacea for all ills, was the catalyst for Marcus Binney's foundation in 1975 of SAVE Britain's Heritage, to campaign powerfully against further loss. It took SAVE to show in 1980 that Scotland was still a land of empty and ruined houses, and in 1986 how vastly we had under-estimated the grievous loss in Wales.

I

Home of the master spy

Langley Park, Buckinghamshire

Langley Park near Slough in Buckinghamshire was a favourite rendezvous during childhood and adolescence. The Harris family, upholsterers of Uxbridge, had long been patronised by Sir Robert and Lady Emily Grenville Harvey. After Sir Robert bloodily shot himself with a revolver in 1931, Lady Harvey was isolated in the house by old age, and died in 1935. They had employed Uncle Sid for a variety of jobs, since as well as being an upholsterer he was a man of all trades.

I was seven in 1938, and little did I know I had already been marked down to continue in the family trade. Even so young, I would go about with Sid, who after Emily Harvey's death continued to do odd jobs at Langley for the trustees of the heir, who lived in South Africa. It was always a thrill to arrive at the tradesmen's entrance to be given tea and buns in the kitchen. Then I would be offered 'treats', which I suspect were contrived by Sid. Perhaps a visit to the Victorian Winter Garden with its greenery and tufa, where I would re-enact

Tarzan, King of the Jungle as shown at the Odeon in Uxbridge on Saturday mornings. There was a walled Chinese or Japanese garden, with fat goldfish in lily ponds, and bronze geese. It was always a thrill to open a scrolly, wrought-iron gate to discover a full-size bronze of a Chinaman seated on an ox, reading a book. Another treat might be the key to the door of the column in the park, to make the exciting ascent of the darkened spiral stair for the view of Windsor Castle. Yet another was to fish for pike, perch and roach in the lake.

Let me describe the place with the hindsight of scholarship. I played in the ancient park of the Kederminsters, who are buried in Langley church. If we are to believe a painted view in the Kederminster Library, installed in the church by Sir John Kederminster in 1615, Langley was an Elizabethan house of surprisingly ambitious size, built in brick soon after 1603. The signal event in its history was the sale of the estate by Lord Masham to Charles, 3rd Duke of Marlborough, whose grandmother, the formidable Sarah, refused him access to Blenheim in her lifetime. Although the Duke built a huge Palladian temple in 1742 designed by Roger Morris – on the site of the late Column – he did not build the new stone house, the one I knew so well, until 1755, to designs by Stiff Leadbetter from nearby Eton. The Duke commissioned Thomas Greening to lay out the Black Park, adjacent to and north of Langley's park, as a fir plantation surrounding a twenty-seven acre lake of ice-cold spring water. Apparently the firs were planted like soldiers on parade, but by 1800 had become an 'impervious forest'. One of the handsome brick quadrangles of stables is Leadbetter's, the other is mostly Jacobean. After the 3rd Duke's death in 1758, the 4th Duke employed Capability Brown to landscape the formal park, plant the perimeter, and make the present lake in 1765. But the Marlboroughs generally used Langley as a transient seat on their way to the Blenheim inheritance, and it only came into its own as a family's chief seat when it was bought in 1788 by Sir Robert Bateson-Harvey. To this family, notably Sir Robert Bateson-Harvey (1825–87) and his successor Sir Robert Grenville Harvey, belong the Blenheim- or Vanburgh-style wings added to the house, the gigantic Anglo-Indian-style viewing column designed by Frederick Pepys Cockerell in 1864, the 1895 Winter Garden attached to the back of the house, and the underground rockwork garden and grotto near the stables. The Oriental gardens must be Robert Grenville's.

When war came in 1939 the gates clanged shut, barbed wire appeared at breaks in the park palings, and soldiers guarded the three entrances to the demesne. First it was HQ Southern Command Home Guard, then it housed Polish units training for D-Day. Out bicycling with Sid, I would ask to be lifted up for an exciting glimpse of those Polish soldiers. The Black Park was utterly isolated, for here was a vast ammunition dump. On Sundays late in the war the sentry at the Shredding Green Lodge would let in the boy of twelve with his rod tied to his cross-bar, to fish in the lower end of Langley's lake, but with dire warnings not to approach the huts outside the ha-ha. Little did Sid or I ever guess as we fished that hundreds of boxes of phosphorus bombs, dumped in the lake, lay below our spinners! They were only discovered in the 1970s. Strange things happened at Langley. I recall two alarming reports in the *Uxbridge Gazette and Middlesex Advertiser*: one, that Polish troops had used the Column for mortar practice, verified years later when under the turf upon which we had walked were found huge accumulations of explosives. The second concerned the sinister discovery on the edge of the park of sacks

34

1. Langley Park, Buckinghamshire, entrance front

2. Langley Park, Buckinghamshire, in the Chinese Garden

of cats' skins. Complaints of missing cats had coincided with the appearance of rabbit in the butchers' shops of Uxbridge, a welcome supplement to our frugal meat ration. It was later rumoured that Mr Piggott the gamekeeper had been a conspirator in this culinary deception.

The estate had already been marked down for acquisition by the Buckinghamshire County Council in 1937. In 1945 they bought the estate for farm management and a public recreation park: on 29 and 30 April 1946 Langley's contents were to be auctioned. Such sales were commonplace at this time, but looked back on with dreaming envy today. I was fifteen, and this was to be my first country-house auction. No longer had I to enter like a tradesman. What satisfaction to see forbidden rooms, and open drawers and riffle through private possessions. Sid possessed a percipient but untutored eye for pictures. I left him in the grand rooms inspecting a French canvas of *Dante Crossing the Styx* (which he bought, and later sold to Wildenstein) and made for the stables, for I had long heard rumours that here was the 'secret' den of Sir Robert Grenville Harvey, an enthusiastic big-game hunter in East Africa and in India, where his sporting expeditions were a smoke-screen for spying on the North West Frontier of India and beyond the Pamirs. His very name evoked the poetry of Empire.

I explored three sides of the stables. In one range a door with a painted notice announcing 'Museum' opened to a vision of a layered and undisturbed accumulation of cupboards and cabinets, shelves and boxes, all under an open timber roof whose beams supported two beautiful wooden skiffs. Here was a higgledy-piggledy collection of coins, fossils, minerals, flint implements from gravel workings at Iver and West Drayton, drawers of spiked butterflies, a banking-up of cases of stuffed birds. In one corner was the improbable sight of the skull and tusks of an

elephant, in another a pile of huge ammonites, and on a shelf a
row of blackened Iron Age pots from a tumulus in the park,
long since lost. I can also recall a bundle of fishing rods, an
ornamental iron and gilt chest that had been dredged up from
the lake, several boxes of books, and in a solitary window some
roundels of yellowish German Renaissance stained glass, reputedly from the Kederminster mansion. In one sense it was a
poor man's *wunderkammer*, reflecting the family antiquarian
curiosity of the past, just like Lord Digby's museum in a garden
temple at Sherborne, or Dickie Bateman's at Old Windsor,
housed in his 'fribble' ornamented farm house, where he might
gaze enraptured at a mummified finger. These were personal
accumulations, enriched by the Grand Tour, the passion of
their owners for local history, and what they picked up as big-
game hunters and colonial servants. Not even *Country Life*
magazine ever published these country-house museums.

I dallied long in Langley's. No one from the bustle around
the house seemed to enter. Yet I had not seen all, and was
puzzled how to gain access to the fourth range until I found an
unassuming door that led me into an enchanting hidden garden – like something out of *Le Grand Meaulnes*. I had entered
the 3rd Duke's huge orangery, or greenhouse. This was Sir
Robert's 'Museum' proper, where was held, as a private
description of Langley stated, 'the best of his COLLECTION OF
HEADS'. Twisting to look upwards, I gasped with amazement at
the stuffed giraffe's head and full neck protruding from the
broken pediment over the inner door. I turned around to see
walls banked with stuffed heads and skins and furs draped on
tables and chairs. On cupboards were many blue, red and
white oriental vases and pots. It could not have been used,
perhaps not ever opened, since Lady Harvey's death, so choking was the musty-fusty smell.

My imagination raced. So here was where the Master Spy had plotted against the Russian Empire. I pushed open a glazed door to the garden, a walled place with dribbling fountain – the water brought all the way from the Black Park – and a wrought-iron gate, aviaries and two vast walled, turfed-over kitchen gardens adjacent. There was an oppressive, deathly silence. I really believe the public attending the auction were unaware of the place, although everything was lotted up. When I crept back to open drawers and cupboards I was transfixed by an object on the table: a full-size black lacquered head of a negro with protruding bright red lacquer lips, black lacquer skin, white-ringed eyes set with a ruby-like jewel, silver ears, and real eye-lashes (or what was left of them) and fuzzy hair. When lifted, it seemed hollow. I eventually called Sid, who found that one ear twisted to allow the cranium to lift up on a hinge: it was a cigar humidor. Having bought it, parcelled up with a dozen other objects in a cardboard box as an extra lot for a few shillings, he discovered a signature and inscription on the silver indicating that it had been made by the famous Parisian designer Ruhlmann in the 1920s. I understand Sid sold it for what was a record price at the time. My purchase was an Egginton greenheart fishing rod.

In the 1950s Sid shared the fishing with Mr Worrell of Amersham, and I was offered the orangery to live in, but gave way to genial entreaties from Delves and Eve Molesworth. He was Keeper of Woodwork at the Victoria and Albert Museum and filled the orangery with his baroque and rococo oil paintings and pieces of German rococo carving and sculpture. In January 1959 I witnessed with Sid the spectacular demolition of Cockerell's column by means of explosives. The locals had gathered in force to see the death, but the constabulary kept us well away. (It occurred to me that one might well have been the same bobby who was frustrated by little Johnny carrying the marble column from Iver Grove one Sunday morning, as I describe later.) A whistle blew, and with a bang and a huge puff of smoke the column disintegrated in the middle, first rising upwards, then crashing down. Against local opposition this disgraceful act of destruction was ordered by the County Planning Officer, Fred Pooley, a modernist who was responsible for the high-rise Council Offices in Aylesbury, widely regarded as a phallic affront in that once lovely low-rise market town. Ironically, the Column may be rebuilt one day, from plans still in the possession of its Uxbridge builders.

I returned to Langley many times, often to see Delves (or Moley, as he was familiarly called) and Eve, once for my fiftieth birthday party, most recently with Eileen, Tim Knox and the landscape historian Todd Longstaffe-Gowan, to find the ancient, blind Eve still in the orangery. Most poignantly, I returned one afternoon to scatter Sid's ashes on the lake to keep a final tryst with the pike his spinner had lured there so often.

2

The vintages were all '45

Shardeloes, Buckinghamshire

B EFORE 1939 HARROW-ON-THE-HILL was a cultural junction.
The Metropolitan Line to Uxbridge with its clean shining
silver trains and stations by Frank Pick represented the age of
Modernism, whereas the line to Chesham and Amersham with
its old-fashioned brown carriages belonged to an older tradition. It was comfy to sit alone surrounded by brown-varnished
woodwork and read the advertisements praising Metroland
and the Chilterns, showing boys and girls, hand in hand with
smiling faces, breasting beechwood uplands. Theirs was a
world innocent of video nasties.

To extend the perimeters of exploration, I would put my
bike in the luggage van. Sometimes, taking the Aylesbury line, I
parked my bicycle at Princes Risborough to catch the
0-4-2C tank engine and carriage on the branch line that hugged
the south escarpment of the Chilterns. Nonchalantly it puffed
and snorted to Chinnor, Aston Rowant, Shirburn and Watling-
ton. Tea followed a browse in a book-shop, then there were

the delights of the return journey, fragrant with the scents that only steam engines produce.

These were halcyon days, when the main road from Amersham to Aylesbury was still rural, and a quiet route for cyclists. Having bicycled from Uxbridge to the Chalfonts and beyond, leaving Amersham, Sid and I came to a porticoed house perched prominently on a hill, looking down on a landscaped lake below: Shardeloes. I later came to regard this view as epitomising the Georgian landscape style of Capability Brown, or of Humphry Repton in the age of Jane Austen. In 1939 the park gates were shut. But it was not the house my attention was attracted by – I was more interested in the possibility of pike or perch than in architecture or gentry. Now, after the war and aged fifteen, I returned to Shardeloes with Sid. I could now appreciate forlorn country houses which had been requisitioned during the war, but not chiefly for their architecture. These immediate post-war years were wonderful for fishermen: so many houses were empty and in a state of limbo, so many lakes had not been fished for five years. The predominantly male fraternity of fishermen had all been called up, and waters were often ours and ours alone. Now was the time, trespass or no! Shardeloes was still in the ownership of the Tyrwhitt-Drake family trustees, who had abandoned it to a maternity home in 1939. As was so often the case with these unwanted houses, it was an oppressively silent place. We discovered the usual decay and signs of abandon: stone and stucco cracked and stained, gardens unkempt, the stables full of paper rubbish and discarded effects. Shardeloes was a classical house built around an early seventeenth-century gabled core. By 1700 an attractive island garden with a fishing pavilion had been built in a formal pool of water, and by 1735 the stables had been built, possibly by Giacomo Leoni, and Charles Bridgeman had laid out a forest garden with avenues striking across the hill. All this changed in 1758, when Stiff Leadbetter built the present house; it was improved by Robert Adam in 1761, and later by James Wyatt, by which time Capability Brown may have landscaped the park.

With our rods tied to our cross-bars, we cycled up the approach to Shardeloes. Sid had organised permission to fish the lake through his other fishing companion, Mr Worrell of Amersham. A keen pike-fisher, he wandered down to the lake formed out of the river Misbourne, once famous for its trout, knowing that in the nineteenth century some local Isaac Walton had pulled a record pike from it. Sid's reward came after our picnic, a good six-pounder. I fished too, but was keener to explore the beckoning house. I made a circuit around to the back and found Adam's grand pedimented Doric Orangery, full of egg boxes, backing onto stables which had seemingly been used for storage. The floor was littered with estate papers belonging to the Drake family. Empty too was the Pigeon House with its quadrant kennels, the bark of hounds no longer to be heard. But how to gain access to the tantalisingly locked house? In a back courtyard I found an unfastened sash window – and in a trice was in the billiard room. I did not know it then, but a terrible mess was most often to be found in the interiors of these abandoned houses – the alien occupants of Shardeloes had been quite respectful, I recall. I trod echoing rooms into which light filtered through closed shutters, my nose wrinkling at that musty smell associated with closure. I noticed neo-classical furnishings, later to be identified as by Adam: two pier glasses and all the pelmets were in position, but the pier tables had inexplicably been removed to the hall. Upstairs the rooms were neatly left. I remember my annoyance at not being able to get into a locked room. It was late afternoon, and as we intended to fish for roach in the cooler evening, I hoisted myself

3. Shardeloes, Buckinghamshire,
from the stables to the side of the house

4. Shardeloes, Buckinghamshire,
the orangery and the back of the house

out of the window and returned to the lake and my rod. I never dreamed that fifteen years later I would arrive here royally, be lavishly dined, and leave in shameful disgrace.

It was 1961, and Gwynn Ramsey, the editor of *Connoisseur*, had asked me to write up Eustace Hoare's flat in Shardeloes. The house had been leased from the Tyrwhitt-Drake trustees by an Ian Mactaggart in 1950 and saved from demolition by Landstone Investments by its conversion into luxurious apartments. Shardeloes was an early demonstration that such unwanted houses could be made commercially viable through conversion. Hoare had recently married Elspeth Cartwright, formerly châtelaine of Aynho; they had taken half the grand state rooms at Shardeloes and had them converted by Patrick Carter and Louis Rich: by a happy coincidence, my father was Rich's upholsterer, and did all the upholstery. I was now an architectural historian, and married to Eileen. 'We are all invited to dinner. It will be a grand affair. Hoare has very good wine,' commented Gwynn, beaming at the prospect.

In contrast to my arrival with Sid in 1946, we now swept up the drive in Gwynn's sleek new white Rolls-Royce, boasting polar bear-fur seat-covers. Standing under the portico to welcome us was Mr Hoare, in a blue velvet dinner jacket, velvet trousers, and blue velvet shoes embroidered with his initials. The company was boring, however, and I was keen to admire the furnishings and paintings which had come from the Cartwright collection at Aynhoe. 'Not now, after dinner,' said Hoare, more concerned to tell us that all the vintages were to be of 1945. We started off with champagne, and I swilled the lovely stuff down. As we talked I cautioned myself: 'Be careful John. Don't get drunk!'

The dinner was delicious, but already I was suffering from

'whirly beds'. A fish mousse came with a Loire (although I never did discover how Mr Hoare managed a '45 for that); the meat was accompanied by no less than a Margaux (of course, '45). Finally, a platter of strawberries, and Château d'Yquem, '45 again. When the strawberries were passed to me, as Eileen told me afterwards, I was oblivious of the fact that I was heaping them on my plate, heaping and heaping, the focus of shocked attention, everyone appalled by my apparent greed. Little did they know I was 'pissed out of my mind'. I passed the platter on to Mrs Hoare with only half a dozen strawberries left. The butler regarded me in consternation, smirking with contempt; Eileen and Ramsey stared in horrified disbelief. I just poured cream on, added piles of sugar, and gobbled up. I was in an alcoholic miasma, and the evening was verging on the disastrous. Port followed; it kills me, but I was fool enough to drink it, delivering the *coup de grâce* to my senses.

Mr Hoare intended to take us around the rooms, pointing out for my special attention the salient points and works of art he wanted discussed and illustrated. But I was out of it. I swayed, and couldn't focus my eyes – except upon one thing: in the library where she was talking to Mrs Ramsey, I was puzzled by the blurred white thing on the floor around Eileen's feet. I swayed over to her and caught her attention; with horror she looked down to see that her petticoat had fallen. Modesty forbids description of her efforts to restore the garment to its rightful place. She was hustled away by Mrs Ramsey, and Mr Ramsey sourly said it was time to leave. We got into his shining car and in silence drove off, our host's last injunction ringing in our ears: 'Remember, this is a home, not a museum!'

Near Northolt the '45 vintages took their revenge: I vomited all over Mr Ramsey's lovely fur seat covers, and Mrs

Ramsey's partly exposed back. He stopped the car, I opened the door, and vomited more on the verge. I will gloss over the pong, the ruined bear skins, and Mrs Ramsey's back. Some days later Mr Ramsey telephoned to say that Mr Hoare had died of a heart attack. Later I wondered how close I had come to being arrested for unintentional homicide.

3

'The key is under the dustbin, sir'

Kenwood House, Hampstead

M Y REFERENCE TO fix the time of this visit to Kenwood is
my friend Keith Blanchard: during the winter of 1946 I
spent a short time staying with him at Wyldes in Hampstead,
where he lodged with Lady Unwin. Keith's architectural training at the Bartlett School necessitated the preparation of a
measured drawing of a building, and he chose the garden front
of Kenwood House, conveniently nearby. An assistant was
needed to drop a lead plummet and measuring line from the
roof of Kenwood.

The house was not then open to the public, but Lady
Unwin made us an appointment with the caretaker. Early in
the morning we arrived, as requested, at a door on the stable
side, to be let in by a caretaking lady of the Mrs Mop sort. We
explained our purpose, were given tea, and then led upstairs,
and further up, to the attic floor and into the roof space. I
remember it was extremely cold. We were taken to a small
door leading onto the roof, and then the cold really hit us.

Mrs Mop retreated, but not before pressing a key into our hands. She was going to shop in Highgate Village: if we finished before she returned, would we let ourselves out and leave the key under the dustbin? Keith retreated with her, to the garden front, to issue commands to me as I leaned over the parapet. The measuring was done in instalments, for fear I might turn into an icy roof statue. During my first break, the bizarre situation at Kenwood was revealed.

The roof space was entirely taken up with Iveagh Bequest pictures. There they all were, with no protection, just one framed canvas leaning against another, not even with sheets of cardboard between them. I lifted one frame back: it was Romney's *Lady Hamilton*; another – Turner's *Lee Shore*; a third – no less than Vermeer's *Guitar Player*. I went rushing back to the parapet, to shout to Keith to come up and see what I had found. He too goggled. He found Frans Hals's *Pieter van der Broecke* and, to our disbelief, Rembrandt's *Self-Portrait*. We were in this house all alone with millions of pounds worth of Old Masters, there for the taking, and the key in Keith's pocket was shortly to be left under the dustbin! But that is not the end of the tale.

Keith decided to make a composite record of front, rear and one side: we must needs make another visit. When Mrs Mop came back from her shopping we asked if we might come again, the day after next, in the afternoon. 'I'm not here till later,' said Mrs Mop, 'but the key'll be under the dustbin.' Key to a fortune! Once again we went up the stairs, into the Iveagh Bequest attic, pulling out pictures, seeing what we could have taken away with ease, Mrs Mop apparently oblivious of what was in her care. What halcyon days of curatorial innocence.

4

A matter of juvenile delinquency

Iver, Buckinghamshire
Delaford Park – Bridgefoot House – Huntsmoor Park –
Richings Park – Iver Grove

FOR PREHISTORIANS IVER and West Drayton are icons spelling out the geological phenomena of the Higher Boyn Hill Terrace of the Thames, their alluvial gravel deposits containing rich remains of early man in the shape of flint implements. To the young John Harris, the existence of gravel deposits meant gravel workings, and thus gravel pits in which he could fish.

I often leaned upon the churchyard wall at Iver, gazing over three parks in a landscape that had hardly changed in a century. My eye, moving clockwise, would first glimpse what remained of the neo-classical villa at Delaford first built in 1802 for Charles Clowes by James Lewis, but rebuilt after a fire in 1845; it then followed the line of the park's retaining wall to Church Lane, to focus at the end upon what is still one of the joys of red-brick Queen Anne: tall Bridgefoot House, fronted by its fine iron gates and the eponymous bridge, all embowered in trees. It was the home of the publisher Martin

Secker, who allowed us to fly-fish the Colne Brook at the rear for very small but lively trout. Beyond could be spied the elms and oaks of the ancient park of Huntsmoor, announced in Iver Lane on the way to Cowley village, where I was brought up, by its Picturesque 'Tudor' lodge. Huntsmoor, demolished in the 1930s, had been acquired by the Tower family, of Weald Hall, Essex, in 1696. This watery demesne was threaded through by the silvery rivers Colne and Frays, from which a channel had been made to create a moated island for the walled kitchen garden. Adjacent were the reflective waters of old gravel pits, notably a particularly fishy one called Denslow's from the name of its owner. Sid had worked in the house in the late 1920s and I can only refer to the place from an old photograph I now have in my possession. When I fished there the brick and stone foundations were still to be seen, as was a gate pier, and broken walls of the kitchen garden. Even today it is still a magical place of brick moats, and a foamy weir near a mill and at the confluence of two courses of the river. In those days it was known only to a few fishermen who sought its perch, roach and dace.

Today, leaning on that churchyard wall has lost its charm. Just below it the M25 cuts its cacophonous swathe, Bridgefoot is isolated, and the park at Huntsmoor has been amputated; Delaford was demolished in 1959. The M25 and the M4 prevent easy access to Richings Park, Iver's other great house. Few sites are so redolent of ancient family, for here was the first Earl Bathurst's beloved 'Riskins', in its day as famous as his Cirencester Park and Pope's Twickenham; the ancient house had passed to Allan Bathurst at Sir Peter Apsley's death in 1691. It was sold to Lord Hertford in 1739, and became renowned under Lady Hertford's tenure for the elegance of her taste in both decoration and ornamental gardening, until

5. Delaford Park, Buckinghamshire, entrance view

6. Bridgefoot, Buckinghamshire,
house and bridge before the M25

7. Huntsmoor Park, Buckinghamshire, the garden front

8. Richings Park, Buckinghamshire, the garden front

her death in 1754. Sir John Coghill followed, and in 1786 the estate was bought by John Sullivan; the house burnt down, and Sullivan rebuilt on a new site. But only later did I come to understand its significance.

In 1947 Richings, recently de-requisitioned by the RAF, may still have been in the ownership of the Sykes family, for whom Sid had worked regularly. Its empty mansion had for me as much attraction as my bobbing float in the long canal. I recollect a tall stone house with an ample bow and flanking pavilions. A bomb had damaged the entrance front, and broken windows and open doors invited entry, offering the thrill of military and RAF graffiti and the detritus of their occupation. It had been the Officers' Mess and HQ, and was surrounded by Nissen huts. Already it exuded the familiar pungent smell of wet and dry rot that I later came to identify with derelict houses. I recall elaborate ornamented 'Adam' ceilings, and in the bow room a chimney-piece with coloured inlays (known as Bossi work). I quizzed the fine mahogany legs of a table with no top or frame. I fished there with Sid, and we would shelter from showers in the house. Often I abandoned my float, yielding to the temptation of the vast mountain of stones dumped in a nearby field from the demolition of John Rennie's Waterloo Bridge in 1934. They were like a giant's building-blocks, the piled masonry towering to make a stepped cubic composition more than fifty feet high. For us village boys it was our private Stonehenge, until the local bobby chased us away.

I returned to Richings in 1994, with Eileen, Tim Knox and Todd Longstaffe-Gowan. Its decayed park and a long canal can be glimpsed after Heathrow, on the north side of the motorway. Cut off by the M4 from the south, the only approach was from Iver, through lanes bounded by smallholdings, detached half-timbered villas of Twenties and Thirties vintage, and fields spotted with the equine accoutrements of those riding schools and pony clubs so ubiquitous in suburbia and the commuter belt. Yet crossing the park boundary was, even now, like leaving one age for another, entering into a time warp. Here were huge ancient and gnarled oaks, of Armada date Todd assured us, the familiar L-shaped and weedy long canal, a walled kitchen garden, and a gardener's house showing much evidence of brickwork dating from the Bathurst period, and even earlier. I stood at first transfixed in thought, my mind returning to 1947. Pointing to a brambly wood I shouted, 'It was there, the house!' Sure enough, we found bricks and cut stone mouldings, and a collapsed cellar poking through the mossy turf – the detritus of the demolition in March 1950. On the edge of this wood was a spooky concrete bomb shelter, its dark entrance disguising a trysting place for village boys and girls. Beyond this were the ha-ha and a stretch of ornamental iron park railing framing a tranquil park, pressing up against the M4. There had been some picturesque Reptonian planting here, perhaps the 'improvements of our own time' mentioned by Lipscombe, the county historian, in 1831. Nevertheless, the configuration of the canal and much of the planting were identifiably of Lord Bathurst's time, designed for him by Stephen Switzer as a *ferme ornée* in the 1710s. The Countess of Hertford has left us ravishing descriptions of her new decorations and her *bergerie* in the gardens. Survivals from the later tenure of the Sullivans were a rusting cast-iron bridge spanning the canal, an ice-house now a lonely hump in the field, and a grand triple-arched stone bridge of the same date as the late lamented neo-classical house. As we surveyed the sward we were puzzled by staked-out areas cleared of grass, and angrily assumed them to be factory plots. After all, Richings is not only under Heathrow's flight path and in the shadow of the intersection of the M25 and M4, but was once designated the site of what was to be the biggest supermarket in Europe. Leaving the time warp, we reflected that soon its memorials of a distant past would be destroyed. We hear it has succumbed to a no less evil – it is a golf course, in servitude to those for whom the first Earl Bathurst might just as well never have been born.

Sid was a great purloiner of bits and pieces from derelict houses. Marble, sculpture, woodwork and a variety of ornaments ended up in his Uxbridge back yard. He bought bits from Delaford, prised out the remaining late eighteenth-century Wedgwood blue and white stained glass with Flaxman style figures from the staircase window at Iver Grove (the other twenty or so panels had already been smashed), and at the cost of a few shillings for the farmer had removed from the garden at Richings a Coade stone tripod.

Iver Grove was another of the village's satellite houses, a red brick villa with a plain pilaster portico built for Lady Mohun in 1722 by the architect John James, although attributed in *The Ambulator* to Sir John Vanbrugh. In 1947 it stood rancid with dry rot. Extending from one side was the later Georgian Great Room added for the Colbourne family, with many neo-Greek plaster bas-reliefs set in the walls. The Great Room, in a state of collapse, had already been relieved of one half of its handsome *giallo antico* yellow marble chimney-piece: young John could achieve symmetry by relieving it of the other. I planned an assault one Sunday morning when few nosey parkers would be about. I carried a canvas bag on my back, and in this put the Ionic capital and slab. When I hoisted the column onto my shoulders, the weight was so great that I realised I would never

9. Iver Grove, Buckinghamshire, side and entrance fronts

be able to walk the mile and a half home. I must go as far as I could, then find somewhere to hide it, to be picked up later. Ten minutes on I was staggering along the road to Iver village, my shoulders aching and bruised. Imagine my horror when, about a hundred yards up the road, I noticed the local bobby coming towards me, pushing his bike. I must look unconcerned. He got near, we passed and nodded good morning, thankfully without comment on his part – but I made the error of glancing back. It was fatal. The bobby had stopped and turned his bike around. Oddly, he didn't shout a warning, but he must have guessed that the yellow marble column could only have come from the empty Iver Grove. Before my eyes flashed the Uxbridge Juvenile Court, and a stern JP sending me down to the Remand Home. In front of me, ten yards away, was a bus stop. 'Not my luck,' I decided, hoping for a bus as I shuffled along, waiting for the tap on the shoulder. With a timeliness that verged on the miraculous, along came the green 458 bus. It stopped, the driver stared, the conductor said 'Gawd!', and I escaped the Remand Home in the nick of time. I can still see the quizzical look on that bobby's face as I looked back at him from the bus. Thank goodness those were the days before mobile phones.

5

Pan with a camera

Painshill Park, Surrey

IT MUST BY now be plain that during the years between the
end of the war and doing my National Service I was something of a nomad, with an almost demonic passion for constant
movement. If I was an architectural historian in the making, it
was because the exploration of abandoned, empty country
houses offered a perfect excuse for indulging this wanderlust.

If I was youth hostelling and hitch-hiking my direction and
destination were entirely arbitrary, depending on the driver. I
was once dropped off by a bridge on the A30 at Cobham in
Surrey. Hesitating, wondering whether to continue, I noticed
by the road an iron gate with a 'Trespassers will be Prosecuted'
notice. The track beyond beckoned, so I climbed over. Immediately I had the sense of a secret place, man-made. The decid-
uous trees exuded lassitude and the sun seemed hardly to
penetrate the chill gloom. At first ascending, I passed a ruined
brick Gothic tower with pointed windows that put me in
mind of Transylvania, and vampires. As a trespasser I was any-

way apprehensive. What was this place? I had no Ordnance Survey map to inform me. The path then descended, below an eminence on which stood a ruined temple – of the 'peripteral' sort, as I was later to learn. It had lost all its side columns, and the capitals of the portico were just hanging from the Doric entablature, a single wooden post used as a prop preventing the pediment from collapsing. This was the Temple of Bacchus, designed by Robert Adam in 1761, and the ornamental landscape garden into which I had intruded, its history then unknown to me, was Charles Hamilton's Painshill. I glimpsed below the path the silvery glitter of the river Mole; descending to it, I marvelled at a huge cast-iron water-wheel next to a weather-boarded pump house – all overgrown and rusted.

In fact I was following the windings of the river that formed the southern boundary of the gardens. I recall passing a brick triumphal arch (this was the Mausoleum), and where the path narrowed I found myself on the edge of a lake clogged with weed. I walked around it to a Gothic ruin spied on the further bank, and the path opened to a clearing with a view of a large timber bridge of six arches. I was just about to venture across when I sensed a presence. I stopped stock-still, almost expecting Pan to emerge from the trees.

What I saw was more mundane: a grey-haired man in a green Loden jacket with a plate camera set up on a tripod, pointing at the bridge. As a youth of sixteen I reckoned him 'elderly'; he was perhaps in his sixties and, by the style of his jacket, German or Scandinavian. He seemed master of his situation, so concentrated was he on his photographic task. I withdrew unseen, and sat down under a tree until he moved away. Passing within ten yards of me without any sign of acknowledging my presence, he followed the path I had taken around the lake, towards the ruined temple and the Gothic tower.

10. Painshill Park, Surrey,
the Gothic Pavilion

11. Painshill Park, Surrey, the Temple of Bacchus

This was my opportunity to cross the rickety bridge onto the island. Here I experienced my first grotto: in retrospect, I wish I had taken home some of the tufa and minerals, as Prince Bentheim of Munster did when he came to admire this garden in 1763. I glimpsed a Gothic temple on the crest of a prominence and, crossing to it, rested under its tottering, open, umbrella-like rotunda. It was now late, and I had to return to the main road along a path which carefully avoided what I later knew to be the neo-classical Painshill House.

I have mentioned that I was in Paris in 1952, after my National Service. My interests were now architecture and the decorative arts. Enrolment at the École du Louvre led to excursions to châteaux and gardens and it was on one of these visits that I discovered the enchanted Désert de Retz, an ornamental landscape garden laid out by Monsieur de Monville between 1774 and 1779. In 1952 it was secret and unknown, to all intents and purposes inaccessible, thanks to a ferocious owner. The Pyramid, Gothic Ruin and Temple to Pan were still there, as was the astonishing Chinese House, teetering on the verge of collapse (the lacquer panels lying about inside), and the Broken Column House retained its neo-classical chimney-pieces, and pieces of smashed furniture.

In 1954 I returned again to Painshill, having read Christopher Hussey's *The Picturesque*. All was the same, except that decay had crept on apace and the Temple of Bacchus had been swept away. On this occasion I found a man of my own age, his paralysed legs in irons, attempting to climb over a barbed-wire fence. It was the indefatigable Alick Barratt, a solicitor with a passion for country houses and gardens: I carried him over, and we have remained friends ever since.

When I was in New York in 1960 at the Avery Library, on

release from the Royal Institute of British Architects, I bought Osvald Sirén's *China and the Gardens of Europe of the Eighteenth Century*, published there by the Ronald Press in 1949 and still one of the most beautifully-produced books ever on gardens. With mounting excitement I found myself looking at familiar images of Painshill and the Désert, in the same state as I had seen them in 1947 and 1952. I was then too callow to recognise the unusual quality of Sirén's photographs, but was drawn to his excellent chapter on William Chambers. This was spellbinding, because the RIBA possessed Chambers's correspondence, and at Avery Library I had found a group of designs by him for chimney-pieces, matching another group in the Metropolitan Museum of Art, where I also discovered his drawings for the Kew Gardens folio of 1763. All this material later contributed to my book on Chambers which was published in 1970.

Because Chambers was an Anglo-Swede born in Gothenberg, I needed to visit Stockholm to research his birth and his affairs with the Swedish East India Company, and the opportunity to meet Sirén was irresistible. After complicated negotiations I went out to Lidingö in 1965, but it was too late. Although his greeting was warm, Sirén at 86 was too old and infirm to respond to my earnest questions. But as I entered his room I was brought up sharp by a flash of recognition: the great and aged scholar sitting in the armchair was no less than the Pan-figure with plate camera I had seen at Painshill.

I have been back to Painshill many times, as a Trustee of the Painshill Trust, and once in Peter Palumbo's helicopter, with Phyllis Lambert and Eileen. Its restoration is one of the triumphs of European garden conservation but, alas, once a garden is restored and tidied up it loses its romantic appeal of decay and ruin.

6

A secret hoard of porcelain

Michel Grove Park and Slindon House, Sussex

I HAVE SAID that Sid was a long-standing member of the Society of Sussex Downsmen. His library of Sussex literature included a scrapbook of drawings by Hieronymous Grimm in which was pasted an old photograph of a water-colour, by Michael Angelo Rooker, of Michel Grove in the 1780s, a lost house I came to know better after meeting Mark Girouard and learning from him of its importance in Elizabethan house-building. Twenty years on, this water-colour turned up in Mr Paul Mellon's collection.

Inspired by the photograph, Sid and I consulted a map. This ancient place was hidden in a fold of the downs below Black-patch Hill, famous for its Neolithic flint mines. In fact we had often passed close by it, since a favoured walk was over Black-patch to Chantry Hill for tea in Storrington. Rooker's water-colour showed Sir William Shelley's romantic house of the 1580s, with its Batty Langley Gothick porches and brick pedimented and pilastered stables that wouldn't have looked out of place in seventeenth-century Holland. 'What was still there?' we both wondered, knowing that the Duke of Norfolk had demolished the house in 1832. A scrutiny of the map showed some buildings there, though perhaps only a farm.

The day was one in early October, and unusual in being a scorcher. From Patching we took the footpath over Patching Hill, and we breasted the summit to discover before us a time-less park redolent of antiquity. Although only the turfed foundations of the house remained, we were well compensated by finding the stables just as they are depicted by Rooker in his water-colour, to the right of the house and as Anglo-Dutch as anything could be. The building was of brick with stone dressings and comprised a temple-like pedimented and pilastered façade of the sort to be seen on canals in Holland or in Dutch topographical paintings. Michel Grove seems to have escaped Pevsner (who was not one for hiking), as also Angmering Park, another downland hideaway skirted by us as we continued on our way through Wepham Woods, dropping down from Warningcamp Hill to Arundel for lunch. That afternoon we thought we might bus out to Slindon.

Before the war Sid had worked for Violet, Lady Beaumont (née Isaacson) at Slindon House. He knew it had been requisitioned, and was still empty: this was our afternoon's prey. First he took me to St Richard's Catholic church with its exquisite – and rare, for England – monument by Thorwaldson, of the Earl of Newburgh who died in 1814. Further along the village street we spied the fifteenth-century lodge, appropriately castellated as befitted what was once a palace of the Arch-bishops of Canterbury. The Gothic gates were padlocked: we must find another way in.

We did, from behind the church, through a hole in the fence. Later I learned that this once attractive old seat had been

12. Slindon House, Sussex, the lodge

13. Michel Grove, Sussex,
Michel Angelo Rooker's view in the 1780s

wrecked by Mervyn Macartney, a graceless architect, in 1921. There were still traces of the palace Archbishop Cranmer swopped with Henry VIII in 1539, but not many. We found ourselves on a lawn (with a dried-up fountain, I think) of tangled thick grass, a high dark hedge as perimeter. The heat of the day seemed to be concentrated on the flint and stone front of the house with its cupola turrets, and to increase the sense of abandon and accentuate the brooding silence.

An open window beckoned. At this point I could refresh my memory from *Country Life* photographs of 1921, but in fact I only remember the Great Hall, as vandalised by Macartney. If Mr Frederick Wootton Isaacson (father of Lady Beaumont) had any say in the matter, he is to be condemned as a man of no taste or judgement for having allowed Macartney to destroy the handsome Georgian interiors in favour of third-rate Jacobethan. However, the nub of this tale concerns another room – a library of white-painted woodwork, the bookcases with cupboards below, maybe Edwardian or Macartney Georgian revival. The shelves were empty except for a large number of copies of *London Illustrated* magazine.

One range of cupboards was locked; the others were empty, but a key in one fitted them all. When we opened the locked range, we gasped. Maybe five were packed with precious porcelain wrapped in newspaper – not just domestic china, but recognised by Sid as French and German eighteenth-century pieces. This astonishing, extraordinary find had the odd effect of making us feel inexplicably guilty. We wanted to leave quickly, before some accusatory hand should appear. We mused: *why* leave such porcelain in the cupboards? Was it a mistake? After all, the rest of the house was empty, just bare boards. I never did discover the reason, and never knew whether my *marchand amateur* uncle subsequently took advantage of our discovery. The genial rogue may well have. My own immediate future held marching and counter-marching in Crookham Barracks parade ground, followed by eighteen months in the Malayan *ulu*.

7

A Polish patriot's place

Dogmersfield Park, Hampshire

IN DECEMBER 1949 came the dreaded buff envelope convey-
ing an ominous summons to Queen Elizabeth Barracks,
Church Crookham, Hampshire, for basic training with the
Royal Army Medical Corps. During the course of those horrible six weeks I sought relief by consulting my lode-star, the
Ordnance Survey map, to discover topographical diversions
and places of refuge. Nearby Odiham village offered book and
tea shops, Farnham its castle and park (years later I discovered
the best place to watch the cricket played next to the castle
was from the top of the castle keep).

Dogmersfield Park intrigued me because it was possible to
follow the tow-path of the disused Basingstoke Canal that
passed through Crookham village and then wound its way
through the park: in fact, the canal had become an ornamental
accessory to the park scenery. I could see that the park had
been huge, two miles around, virtually enwrapped by the
canal. The church and house seemed to be in a disparked area,

white on the map rather than grey. I could explore the park, join the canal once again, and end up at Odiham for tea. My memories of January 1950 are now enriched by the later scholarship of Mark Girouard and Howard Colvin, but even today Dogmersfield is a tantalisingly unknown house and estate.

The Tudor house in which Edward Goodyer died in 1686 was the same that had received its window glass in 1573. The marriage of Martha Goodyer to Ellis St John brought the house to this branch of the St John family, and it was Martha and Ellis who by 1728 had sumptuously rebuilt the north and west fronts in a brick Palladian style. Ellis's son Paulet later dotted the park with ornamental follies, some possibly by the astronomer-architect Thomas Wright. An early painting and Isaac Taylor's map of 1759 show a belvedere, a Palladian bridge, an arch, a Gothic tea-house, and a gabled folly, the scene also painted about 1747 by James Seymour in a hunting prospect. The north front then looked out over a huge expanse of pre-Capability Brown, naturalised lawn, reaching from the walls of the house to the edge of the lake. Aligned eastwards of the house Seymour showed grand Georgian stables, and the medieval church and village.

It was a cold wintery Sunday when I left camp, eventually to climb up the embankment of the canal and make for the church – not Benjamin Ferrey's opulent All Saints of 1843, built a mile to the north by St John-Mildmays of the day on the western reaches of the park, but the medieval church rebuilt in 1806 in brick, with crenellated tower, plain two-bay nave and simple pointed windows. What dereliction met my gaze! The windows of the church were smashed, the walls embowered in ivy, the west door boarded up. I climbed through a window, skirted broken pews, and in the dark nearly fell into an open vault – I suppose it belonged to the St

John-Mildmays. The vault slab had been levered up, and when my eyes got used to the gloom I saw a jumble of opened coffins. It was too spooky even for 22318793 Acting Unpaid Lance Corporal Harris to contemplate for long, although I did think of taking a skull back to my barrack-room mates.

From the church the drive led straight towards the house, but first I must spy out the land by discreet circumambulation, like a predator stalking its prey. What I initially found was not Georgian – a walled kitchen garden, with an Edwardian green-house, laid out as I later discovered by Sir Henry St John-Mildmay sometime before 1901. During the Second World War vegetables had completely supplanted flowers for the house, and the greenhouse had been allowed to rust and decay. I was alarmed to see three tethered goats – evidence of human presence. So I warily approached the back of the house, the south front, where much Victorian and Edwardian building had taken place (as I later learned, William Burn made many alterations in 1860).

Broken windows, open doors and clogged gutters, the usual tally of woe owners could expect to find upon derequisition: if someone cared for those goats, it was not from here. I was entering the back quarters of a forlorn and empty house. There was a suggestion of an earlier Tudor courtyard range, rebuilt on the north and west sides with the addition of new and resplendent brick ranges. It seemed obvious that the intention had been to rebuild the whole, but that the scheme had got no further and been given up.

As I passed from room to room I observed the familiar detritus of transient wartime occupation: notice boards and signs in Dutch and Polish, iron bedsteads, broken tables, smashed windows, sad bathrooms with rusting fittings, the baths filled with rubbish, disgusting clogged toilets. I remember

14. Dogmersfield church, Hampshire, from the south-west

15. Dogmersfield Park, Hampshire, after the fire, 1981

two grand rooms in the 1728 range, each with fine chimney-pieces, one with caryatids or terms, and rich plastered ceilings. When I refreshed my memory from photographs recently, I was reminded of the baroque Palladianism of James Gibbs or Giacomo Leoni. Indeed, one ceiling was in the style of the Italian stuccoists Artari and Bagutti. The rest, notably the staircase area, displayed a dark brown Edwardian decor. I retain a clear and powerful recollection of what I found behind doors upstairs. A large attic room with a sloping ceiling was ornamented on one wall by a huge and startling coloured chalk head of a man wearing a Polish military cap. He seemed familiar, and I later recognised him as General Sikorski, the Polish patriot tragically killed (or assassinated) during the war. Nailed to the plaster above his head was a faded, crumbling laurel wreath: this had been a shrine for the Polish airmen billeted here. Another door led to a room used to store old suitcases and piles of mildewed books, a last refuge for family mementoes. In it was an Arts and Crafts white-painted wooden chimney-piece with beautiful eighteenth-century Delft tiles, every one of which had been individually and systematically smashed. Downstairs, I found the door in the 1728 front standing open. This front had statues, maybe of Coade stone, in niches. I turned to look out over an English landscape park remodelled (after Seymour painted his sporting view) by William Eames, the landscape gardener who worked from the 1760s, in the manner of Capability Brown. However, his was not the earlier ornamental park, nor the bill submitted between 1790 and 1800 for 'Pulling down ornamental building in Park, £500'.

The wintery dusk was closing in, a tour around the lake beckoned, and so did tea in Odiham. But first I must examine Benjamin Ferrey's church, where some St John monuments from the 1806 church had been relocated. *En route* I saw a small red brick gabled pavilion, a sort of folly I thought, where two men were gardening. I paused, but felt unwilling to intrude. Perhaps I should have done so. A few years later, returning to the Hunting Lodge in a different capacity, I saw those two men again: one was the decorator John Fowler, who bought this folly in 1947, the other his friend Ian McCallum, then of the *Architectural Review* – both, now, of late lamented memory.

Poor Dogmersfield. Its fate typifies the demise of landed families. The Mildmay estate of 2,375 acres had been broken up in the 1930s. Reed's School arrived in 1955, shortly followed by De La Salle College, then by Danehill Preparatory School, from 1972 until 1981, when fire completely gutted the Georgian ranges. Don't bother to go there now. It is the headquarters of a business concern who upon enquiry proved to be utterly uninterested in the history of their place. The magic departed with the Poles and the Dutch. And as for once rural and lovely Odiham, don't bother with it, either: it has been consumed by its neighbour, the new Basingstoke, and when I was there last seemed a favoured venue for noisy ton-up boys from that shattered but once delightful Hampshire market town.

8

An impending need for a change of address

Badger Hall, Shropshire

IN 1952, HOME from Paris, out of work and on the dole, I was on my travels. A long hitch had taken me into Shropshire, and I was staying at the Wilderhope Manor youth hostel. One warm evening I saw what I soon discovered to be Badger Hall, invitingly sun-dappled across an unkempt park. Investigation was imperative. As I approached, the dried-up fountains, shaggy grass, empty windows and air of general decay all bespoke a terminal case.

But I was not alone. From a French window in a projecting conservatory, a man watched. I confidently walked towards him. 'What do you want?' he demanded; when he discovered that my interest was friendly, he told me the house was by the architect Wyatt, and indeed the first (1954) edition of Howard Colvin's *Biographical Dictionary of British Architects* stated, under James Wyatt, that it had been built 'for Isaac Hawkins Browne, 1779–83'; in the 1978 edition, the entry was modified to 'remodelled for'. Photographs indicate that the alter-

16. Badger Hall, Shropshire, from the garden

17. Badger Hall, Shropshire, from Wyatt's dining-room

ation was correct: the west front with its channelled pilasters
seems to be of the 1740s, and I can remember noticing at least
one rococo ceiling when the caretaker took me through the
house.

The estate had belonged to the Capel Cures, and although
there had been a sale in September 1945, many objects survived from the remarkable Italian Renaissance collections
formed by Robert Cheney. I noticed an Italian Renaissance-
style fireplace in the evocatively-named Museum Room, still
with its Virgin and Child terracotta in the overmantel, while
in the conservatory from which I had been spotted was a medley of antique, Renaissance and nineteenth-century sculptures,
including a very important Venetian well-head and an antique
Roman funeral stele. Wyatt had formed a suite of three grand
rooms on the east front, comprising library, drawing room and
dining room, and put in a new staircase. Looking back, I can
only fulminate that all this was needlessly destroyed. The dining room with its barrel-vaulted ceiling, its inset paintings and
screened apse still with its elegant fitted Wyatt serving table,
was a neo-classical masterpiece. From Colvin's third (1995)
edition of the *Dictionary* I note that the same Edward Haycock
who remodelled Onslow Hall in 1815 altered Badger for this
Robert Cheney in 1849. His, perhaps, was the ground-floor
library with grand late-classical caryatid chimney-piece.
Upstairs in the bedrooms were several rococo chimney-pieces,
and one by Wyatt. In the garden at the rear a nineteenth-
century fountain was topped with a Renaissance marble putto.
The evening was drawing in, and I had to leave. I turned back
to look at the lovely garden front in the dusk, and sighed: the
caretaker had told me the house was scheduled for demolition
in a month's time. The address is now 19 Badger Fields. What
bathos!

9

The gift of a Burke's *Peerage*

Breakspears House, Middlesex

I N MY ADOLESCENCE the village of Harefield on the very bor-
ders of Middlesex, west of Uxbridge, was an icon for two
reasons: for the fishing, and for the delight of Harefield church
with its funerary monuments. Sid and I frequently wandered
the six miles of that delightful watery valley from Uxbridge to
Rickmansworth that marks the boundary between Middlesex
and Buckinghamshire. Several water-courses could be followed and fished: the rivers Frays and Colne, the Misbourne
branching off towards the Chalfonts to refresh that very fishy
lake in Chalfont Park, and the Grand Union Canal. The rich
alluvial deposits meant a network of gravel pits around Rickmansworth, and these waterways were bisected by the pre-
Beeching branch line of the Great Western Railway from its
terminus at Uxbridge to join the Metropolitan Line at Denham. The line was laid on a raised embankment, and below it
on land belonging the Sanderson wallpaper factory was an old
disused canal wharf, producing record local tench. The rurality

of these border lands has survived in a surprising way: fifty years on, the M40 and the newer M25 form a *cordon sanitaire* round them. An extension to the Western Avenue became the Uxbridge Bypass (and now the M40), crossing our fishing valley by a spectacular pre-war concrete viaduct, and from it one has provocative glimpses of the mansions on Harefield's edge, not least Harefield Place, built by Sir Roger Newdigate in 1786. These were Newdigate lands, and few churches in the country can better the glorious collection of family monuments in Harefield church.

Today architectural historians associate Sir Roger Newdigate, amateur architect and man of taste who died in 1806, with the family seat at Arbury in Warwickshire. But Harefield boasts all the earlier family monuments from the fifteenth century onwards – and by what sculptors! – William Stanton, Grinling Gibbons, John Michael Rysbrack, William Hayward, John Bacon. And there are other contenders in the matter of funerary display: the romantic tomb of Alice, Countess of Derby (1637), who held the manor in an interim of Newdigate possession, and in the north chapel the monuments of the Ashbys of Breakspears, also from the fifteenth century, notably the noble monument of Sir William Ashby by Sir Robert Taylor, 1769.

I returned from Paris in 1952 to find that Sid was now excited by fishing the Colne where it encircled Denham Court on its arcadian island. Dryden wrote of this place that 'Nature has conspired with art to make the garden one of the most delicious spots in England', likening it to Alcinous's garden, and it was a joy to find virgin waters free of interference by competitive Isaac Waltons. When we first fished there the house was a refuge for naughty boys, I believe. It was partly in a plain Georgian style, but with remains from the seventeenth

18. Breakspears, Middlesex, the garden front

century. One lunchtime I left Sid, after a morning's fishing, to seek out Breakspears House. Remembering the Ashby tombs at Harefield, I was curious to see the house itself, where Nicholas Breakspear, as Pope Adrian IV (1154–9), reputedly lived. Certainly a William Breakspear was there in 1376.

Comparing the old Ordnance Survey map I used then, corrected to 1948, with the present 1981 edition (now called Landranger – as if Ordnance Survey was not good enough), I find that the land configuration of my first approach to Breakspears is still identifiable. I walked by the Colne to the railway bridge, crossed that and then the canal bridge, and here enjoyed a little *frisson*: from the railway embankment I noticed a couple on the edge of a wood below, the man furtively casting his eyes around; they did not see me, as I watched them engage in copulation. After this somewhat disturbing intermission I took a lane to Dewes Farm and Highway Farm, and found the lodge to Breakspears' old southern drive. Today

Dewes Farm is no more, and Harefield Moor, flooded with reservoirs, is more watery than ever.

I must explain that my memory of Breakspears in 1952 is of generalities rather than detail. I arrived at the garden or south front and remember long red-brick ranges, hipped roofs and some bulgy bay windows. I could sense it was seventeenth-century. I also remember a shell hood door on another front, and an extraordinary growth of creepers everywhere. Pevsner, who came here in 1950, gave it seven lines, and can never have been inside – but then, he was not one for climbing through windows. By contrast, in her *London 3: North West* (1991) Bridget Cherry gives it an historically useful thirty-nine lines. Thanks to her I can observe in retrospect the detail of what I saw, how the house was extensively remodelled inside by its owner, Alfred H. Tarleton, from 1887, with a drawing room and smoking room of 1899, accompanied by much re-jigging of early panelling and chimney-pieces.

The place was abandoned. I climbed through a window to find an ordered chaos. A billiard table had lost its legs, just sawn off – I suppose to warm an airman's hands, for this house was near RAF Uxbridge. In the stair hall were several dustbins full of broken china, clothes and paper, and in another ground-floor room empty metal boxes of an ammunition-holding sort were piled one upon another. Upstairs – access by way of a handsome seventeenth-century oak baluster stair – I recollect nineteenth-century parts, notably a library. Was it white-painted wood? My memory is clear about the hundreds of books scattered across the floor, leftovers from some sale which today would feature as desirable lots in any London auction. I filched a Burke's *Peerage* of 1937, and have it still: thank you, descendants of the Tarleton occupancy.

There is one other event to relate. I walked through most

of the house, came to servants' quarters and paused, amazed, at a kitchen. It had been made redundant by the Tarletons in favour of a more modern one, and simply abandoned, a perfectly-preserved entity from the eighteenth century, like those at Calke in Derbyshire or Erddig in North Wales, or the tragically dispersed one at Casewick in Lincolnshire. When Breakspears became an Old People's Home in 1956, a junk merchant in Slough cleared everything out and all the Georgian equipment was dispersed.

As I left, Burke's *Peerage* weighed heavily on me. On the way out, by a lodge built in 1904, I found the early Tudor dovecote. I left Burke inside, and picked it up on my bicycle a week later. I have recently learned that W.S. Gilbert wrote *The Yeomen of the Guard* here. I cannot imagine what Pope Adrian IV would think of the new Breakspears Crematorium.

10

A room that may never have been

Shurland Castle, Kent

WHAT I DISCOVERED at Shurland Castle on the Isle of Sheppey was a still-life of such improbability that it defies explanation, unless as an apparition. I knew the place only as a Tudor castle, and in 1953 there was no enlightening John Newman's *Kent* to fill out its history, and tell me that Henry VIII came here in 1532. My route to it was via Sitting-bourne, changing to the Sheerness branch line and a welcoming and aromatic steam-engine which took me to Queensborough. I had shepherd's pie in a pub there, then walked the five miles to Eastchurch, in sight of the famous Battle of Britain aerodrome and with the bleak marshes of the Isle of Sheppey on my right. In the church I wondered if the Gabriel Livesey and his wife (1620s), and the other Liveseys who are entombed here, had lived at Shurland Castle. The Castle was just off the lane (now the holiday tripper's A250, leading to Leysdown-on-Sea), and I faintly remember approaching it across a flat plain. There was the Castle, sited

19. Shurland Castle, Kent, entrance front

20. Shurland Castle, Kent, diagonal view through offices

upon a ridge overlooking a landscape as yet undisclosed to me: what I saw was the west range of an early sixteenth-century Tudor courtyard house, a brick building, its two octagonal towers with a white staccato pattern of stone coigns, Tudor and Georgian windows, and a large arched central doorway, padlocked. The whole of the north-east angle of this range, towards a grouping of farm buildings, had collapsed. Broken and open windows beckoned, within was a passage strewn with the detritus of evacuation, a stair to be mounted, and then *The Room*.

Lit by two windows of broken glass, it generally seemed more Georgian than earlier but it was plain, with an early nineteenth-century ceiling that had mostly collapsed on to the floor and a simple stone Tudor chimney-piece. On one wall a seventeenth-century tapestry hung in such tatters that the composition could not be identified. Two other walls had green damask, but most had been ripped away. Even in such decay these three walls seemed Edwardian in the making. Against one stood a large French provincial armoire, missing its carved wooden doors. When I turned to look at the door-way to the room I couldn't imagine how it had been got in. Across the floor was strewn a medley of broken bits of furniture – a gilt ballroom chair, the back of a walnut chair maybe about 1730, a gilt curtain pole, and a broken slab of rather pretty marble. All were covered with lumps of fallen plaster. The most bizarre item in this bizarre room was a huge nineteenth-century gilt picture frame, missing its picture, that had been buckled into a corner. It was similar to the scene I had encountered in the Column House of the Désert de Retz the year before, and I recollected both when I visited Uffing-ton in 1958. To each side of *The Room* I found others, empty but covered in the graffiti that betrayed military wartime occupation – Shurland was used by the RAF from the aerodrome at Eastchurch.

My imagination raced in *The Room*, trying to reconstruct its why and wherefore. Did the last owners consign their valuables here, tapestries, pictures, furniture, hoping that locked away they might survive requisition? Did they never return, dead perhaps on some distant battlefield? It was even more puzzling when I later discovered from the public library in Sheerness that by local repute the place had been occupied by tenant farmers, who probably couldn't tell a seventeenth-century tapestry from a grain sack. Moving from the centre of this stage to draw back the shutters more fully, shutters carved with a simple shallow rococo pattern, I stared in gasping disbelief at what I saw outside: at the bottom of a decline to sea-level stretched, not battalions of soldiers on parade, but battalions of holiday caravans – seemingly all the two miles to Warden and Warden Point. I began to wonder whether *The Room* would still exist once I had left it: and I did so hurriedly, for the spookiness was acute.

11

A mentor for all aspirants

A day at Hungershall Lodge, Kent

WHEN I WAS in Malaya between 1950 and 1951 I acquired *Historic Cyprus* (1936) by one Rupert Gunnis, little anticipating what that name would come to mean to me. It was in 1954 that Howard Colvin told me I should meet Rupert Gunnis, whose *Dictionary of British Sculptors, 1660–1851* had appeared the previous year. So I wrote to him at Hungershall Lodge near Tunbridge Wells.

Never did any youthful aspirant receive such a warm reply: 'Come down to Tunbridge Wells as soon as you can. Next Saturday?' Followed telephone calls, train times, then there at the appointed hour in the station forecourt was Rupert, who was to become my mentor. He was then 55 years of age: alas, I was to enjoy him for only another eleven years. His face was soft and rounded, his eyes blue and twinkling. Dressed in conventional tweeds, his patrician, county look belied his true character.

Hungershall Lodge was a plain, stuccoed, plate-glass-windowed late-Regency house of asymmetrical plan on the edge of Hungershall Park just beyond the Common in a large flower garden. Its undemonstrative exterior gave no hint of the wonderland inside. I already knew a few collectors' houses: Geoffrey Houghton Brown's painterly amalgam of decorative objects woven around Boulle furniture in Thurloe Square, Paul Wallraf's glitzy treasure-trove in Grosvenor Place. But Hungershall was different. The rooms were compendiums of such objects as can hardly be imagined in an age when Renaissance 'Cabinets of Curiosity' are as distant from us as Horace Walpole's Strawberry Hill.

Only from Bruce Bailey's photographic record is it possible to reconstruct the first mind-blowing impression of entering Rupert's house. Hall, ante-room, double drawing room, dining room and many upstairs rooms were crammed from floor to ceiling with every imaginable type of work of art or curiosity: paintings, drawings, bronzes, marbles, terracottas, an abundance of wax portraits, miniatures, engravings, needlework, glass paintings, silver, layer upon layer. It was like being wrapped in an exotic and colourful carpet. It must also be said that they were the decorative cocoon of a most relaxing and comfortable ambience. But there was more – Rupert's library rooms, his 'dynamo' as he called them, full of books on topography, genealogy, architecture, sculpture and archaeology, and impregnated with that heavenly musty aroma of old bindings. Overall there floated always the fragrance of orchids selected from the orchid house. Rupert's was a bewitching catholicity of taste.

There was a strict routine to be followed: first sherry and conversation, which Rupert might laughingly begin with 'Now, who have we got to hate today?' This involved much ribaldry and many mischievous tales. Rupert could be outrageous. He would have enjoyed taking on Political Correctness and feminists. He loved to fulminate jocularly about current concerns. He frequently took a swipe at the National Buildings Record, blaming poor 'Farthing' (Cecil Farthing, distinguished past Director of the NBR) for not photographing a country house before its demolition; or at Ministry investigators whom he thought spent more time dealing in antiques than listing buildings. Such outspokenness cost him dear. He was anathema to Sir Francis Watson, Director of The Wallace Collection, a great authority on French furniture and another mentor of mine, because of his critical review of C.F. Bell's monograph on the sculptor Thomas Banks. Bell held that the Chute monument at The Vyne was by Banks, but Rupert attributed it to Thomas Carter (probably correctly, as we now surmise). As Bell was Watson's gay friend, Watson always saw to it that Rupert was blackballed by the Society of Antiquaries, though few deserved to be a member more than Rupert. It was a shabby episode in the Society's history.

Rupert Gunnis's was the happy life of an antiquarian (as well as a good JP), making progresses around Britain, often with Howard Colvin, examining cold and dusty muniment rooms in country houses, or propping ladders up on church monuments to discover signatures. He had many a strange encounter. One Sunday morning at Calke in Derbyshire he found the gateway to the churchyard in the park locked; he then witnessed the arrival of the priest and a line of tenants, more old than young, each bending down to crawl through a hole in the fence because Calke's owner Mr Jenney (later – 1961 – Harpur-Crewe) refused to unlock the churchyard gate.

After drinks we would progress upstairs to the main library room, presided over by Kathleen Mann's portrait of Rupert as

21. Hungershall Lodge, Kent, entrance hall

22. Hungershall Lodge, Kent,
small library with portrait of Rupert Gunnis

a young man. 'Now it's question time,' Rupert would say: this was also routine. The callow scholar was expected to bring as many questions as possible. 'Where did the second Lord Grantham live?'; 'Where is Dandelion?'; 'Is this drawing by Edward Pierce?'; and so on. Woe betide the scholar if there *were* no questions. Rupert would either get up to look for the book himself, or else say, 'Room 2, shelf 14 b, 1776 *Baronetage*'. An hour would pass as minutes. It was all thrilling.

Then followed lunch prepared by his housekeeper Mrs Lucy, always the best of traditional English cooking – very good lamb and tasty apple pie, and usually cider to drink – and the surprise, if you weren't expecting it, of being served by the handsome Mamuk Kemal, in Turkish dress. Kemal was Rupert's manservant and friend, brought back from Cyprus when Rupert resigned from the Consular Service for certain archaeological misdeeds. Kemal served him faithfully to the end of his days and retired to run a small chicken farm, from which I continued to obtain delicious eggs.

After lunch an afternoon trip in the car was mandatory. The destination might be the site of a demolished house or, as in 1963, the burnt-out remains of Syndale, a Cromwellian giant order house: smoke was still rising from the blackened shell. A frequent stop was Lord de L'Isle at Penshurst, or Lord Camden at Bayham Abbey, or Nellie Ionides at Buxted Park. Buxted was always a treat, for it involved both a scrumptious tea and architectural salvage-spotting: a chimney-piece from Clumber, the staircase from the Burlingtonian 30 Old Burlington Street, stone terms from Sir John Vanbrugh's Ashley Park, urns and balustrade from Isaac Ware's Chesterfield House, or bits and pieces from Robert Adam's Arlington Street and Matthew Brettingham's Norfolk House – all very cleverly assembled by Basil Ionides, an architectural decorator if there ever was one.

We made two excursions to Ashburnham Place before the dreadful auction of its contents, accumulated since medieval times. I wanted to witness its demolition in 1959, but Rupert said, 'No: if you do, I won't speak to you again' – so bitter was he that this precious artistic entity had not been kept intact.

Ashburnham was just one (if the worst) of a series of losses and dispersals. Rupert had witnessed the demolition of James Wyatt's Lee Priory in 1953, and we both drove to look at the outside of Belvedere, near Erith, before it went in 1957. After the demolition Rupert found there were only a few snapshots in the National Building Record's file, and this sparked off further fulminations against the Record. A rule had been introduced that if the photographer found images already in the file there was no need to make a further survey, and in consequence dozens of houses were lost without adequate record. Of course, the NBR could not cope with that phenomenon of 1955, when one house was demolished every two and a half days. I can just imagine Rupert's splenetic reaction to the NBR's equally idiotic removal in 1992 to Swindon, although fortunately its housing makes up for its isolation. As I recollect, far the most terrifying was the ire he felt towards the wretched owners of Brightling Park in Sussex, when against his advice they destroyed the wondrous Palladian Great Room.

Eileen and I spent the day of 23 July 1965 at Hungershall Lodge. At the end of such a day we always liked to walk to the station, on the way stopping at the bookshop (Hall's) of Mr Pratley, one of Rupert's trustees and the source of many of his books. Rupert seemed unsettled that day and, unusually, insisted on taking us to the station. He pressed us to spend the following weekend with him, we declined, and he pressed us again more forcibly – but we had an unavoidable dinner date. The next Saturday night we were awoken near midnight by a loud, insistent knock at the door. It was ambulance men who stated that they had been summoned to my address, which they insisted was 16 Limerston Street. I sent them across the road to 16 The Sand Hills, but there had been no call from there. They departed, puzzled, and I returned to bed. At a quarter to two I awoke shaking and in a muck sweat. Eileen informed me that I had been nightmarishly shouting. She calmed me down, I gasped, then fell into a profound sleep. Later that morning the telephone rang, and I learned that at midnight the Duke of Wellington at Stratfield Saye, where Rupert had spent the weekend, had noticed his old friend nodding in a strangely comatose state. Alarmed, he called a doctor, but at a quarter past two Rupert passed away in his armchair.

12

Nearly a Catholic mass

Onslow Hall, Shropshire

I HAVE SEEN houses actually in a state of *rigor mortis* – Burwell in Lincolnshire, Warnford in Hampshire, Fairford Park in Gloucestershire, and Onslow Hall in Shropshire. Touring the county in 1954, Pevsner saw the last-named, but never gained access, and by the time *Shropshire* was published in 1958 a footnote announced its demolition. In fact it went soon after he saw it. My going there was quite accidental: Geoffrey Houghton Brown was staying at Chirk Castle, and it was my intention to spend the weekend in Shrewsbury. We called upon an antique dealer in the town, who told us Onslow was coming down. There might be stuff for sale – we should see it. So we did.

The house had two lodges on the Welshpool road, west of Shrewsbury: as we arrived, out of one, ominously, came a lorry. We were confronted by an attractive landscaped park, and Onslow, in the process of dismemberment. We met someone who may have been Mr Wingfield, the owner; he later

23. Onslow Hall, Shropshire, portico front in demolition

24. Onslow Hall, Shropshire, rear of house in demolition

told me the house had been a French girls' school during the war. The third (1995) edition of Howard Colvin's *Dictionary* notes that Edward Haycock of Shrewsbury remodelled Onslow for John Wingfield, *c.* 1815; he was probably responsible for the giant fluted Greek Doric portico and front. It was a bare, gloomy and somewhat unlovable house, lacking exterior relief. To one side, as I remember, was a large wing of uncertain date. The roof had been taken off and the interior dismantled; chimney-pieces lay on the lawn with the iron balustrades of the stair, cut up into sections. As we walked through the spaces – no longer rooms, for most of the floorboards had been taken up – in fear of our lives from falling masonry, it seemed obvious from the exposed walls that later work had enclosed an earlier house. One wooden chimney-piece was prettily rococo, and this Geoffrey haggled to buy for Felix Harbord.

The staircase had once been magnificent, an Imperial stair rising up to an arcaded landing, the walls either marbled or of scagliola. We had been warned by an overseer that we entered the house at our peril, and it was here that Geoffrey nearly got killed. He stopped to look up at the exposed brick carcass of the staircase, oblivious of the men up among the arcades, picking away at its life: a huge piece of stonework crashed in front of him, but evoked no more than a deprecating smile and 'Oh! Nearly a mass.'

A house in process of dismemberment is more affecting than one that is gone, leaving an empty site. I wandered down to the lake and thought of Piscator Sid, for that weedy mere breathed pike. A tank engine and two carriages chuffed nonchalantly and picturesquely along a branch line from Shrewsbury, making for Shrawardine and into the Welsh Marches.

We then left, pressing onwards with a diversion to Woodhouse, near a large airfield, but found the Robert Mylne house uninhabited and inaccessible. I came this way another time with Christopher Gibbs, *en route* to the Sweeney Hall sale near Oswestry, and once again with Gervase Jackson-Stops on the way to Powis. Gervase and I wondered if Pevsner had suffered a paper-loss hereabouts: he described Ruyton-XI-Towns, but not Ruyton Park or Boreatton Park, or Tedsmore Hall, or Pradoe House with its church, or Grimpo church. Had the little pieces of paper detached themselves from the clipboard and blown away?

13

For Aquascutum overcoat
read army issue

Lydiard Tregoze, Wiltshire

I RECOLLECT A story Rupert Gunnis told of visiting St John Vernon Henry, 6th Viscount Bolingbroke, at the Dorset house to which he decamped after selling Lydiard Tregoze, his family home. He was a scion of a family of ancient lineage even in Shakespeare's day – but, Rupert exclaimed, 'He was orf his rocker!' When Rupert knocked at the door, a head appeared out of an upper window and commanded him to 'Push open the door. I'll be down in a tick.' Rupert did so, and waited in the stair-hall for an unconscionably long time. Then he heard a shuffling: looking up towards the landing, he could only stare speechless at the apparition of the dotty peer dressed in his ermine robes with coronet perched on his head and accompanied by a maid. Rupert told me this tale in response to mine involving Lydiard and the Aquascutum overcoat.

Once this St John had left Lydiard in 1939 to indulge his dottiness in Dorset, only the great accumulation of family monuments in the church remained as mementoes of the family's noble lives at their noble seat. Neither the urban spread of Swindon nor the new County Borough of Thamesdown had yet come about, but tentacles were already reaching out to rural Lydiard on its escarpment only three miles to the west. Not surprisingly, greedy town planners had long coveted the estate for a recreational park. Now it was theirs.

Responding to its change of ownership and use, its perhaps uncertain future, Christopher Hussey wrote two articles on Lydiard for *Country Life* in April 1948. The church crammed with monuments, huddling with the mansion on its hill, the family's long tenure, the empty echoing rooms, the sheer beauty of the architecture and decoration of an unquestioned Great House, evoked in him an emotional response. His words conspired to tantalise, and were later a powerful incentive to me to visit the house. Also, and even more to the point, it was a case where the family papers had reputedly been consigned to the bonfire (by the Viscount), and the name of the architect was long debated. It still is. Was it Roger Morris, or William Kent? What a crucial question for a young architectural historian. I just had to see the place, and so I wrote to Swindon Council.

I don't seem to remember ever bothering about weather or the time of year in those days – it was late November of 1954. A letter arrived at 20 Thurloe Square commanding me to present myself at the house at two in the afternoon and ask for the caretaker. I was warned that the builders were in. I left Paddington on the Great Western Railway in flurries of snow and arrived at Swindon in an alarming snow-storm, and I had heard on the wireless that the Thames around Cricklade was in flood. I alighted in what was still an old nineteenth-century railway town with rural overtones, rather than the high-tech city of today. The medieval centre was still identifiable. The Lawn, Swindon's grand house, had been demolished as recently as 1952. I was early and lunch beckoned, in the Railway Hotel. All I can remember of that lunch was putting pepper on my melon instead of sugar – not an auspicious omen – and when I left the hotel the snow was even worse.

At the bus station they said I would have to go towards Lydiard Millicent and ask to be dropped at the Lydiard Tregoze turn. The snow was now blinding, and the bus conductor, clearly solicitous of my situation, left me standing at the corner of a lane, tightly buttoned up in a new, heavy and expensive Aquascutum overcoat. I was very proud of this overcoat for, hanging down below my knees, it possessed a certain old-fashioned 1930s look. On my companionable Ordnance Survey map I had already noticed that the lane dropped into a valley and crossed a stream, a branch of the river Ray, itself a tributary of the Thames eight miles to the north near Cricklade. In retrospect, I should have found this ominous. As I descended towards the bridge I was so blinded by snow that all I could see was swirling water. It was in fact a foot above the road, and impassable. From the map I could see that the house was near, just across a field, so I retreated and attempted a diagonal approach. Off the road I sank into snow above my shoes, then above my ankles, but could scarcely turn back, in blinding snow and with no means of returning to Swindon. I thought all the time of Scott or Shackleton as I squelched along like a walking snowman. It was freezing. Suddenly, it seemed as though the earth had given way, and I sank above my knees in mud and water: even now, forty-three years on, I can relive my fright lest I should sink further still, and drown. But I stumbled on through water and slush, weighed down by that damned, sodden Aquascutum. Then to my relief I sensed

25. Lydiard Tregoze, Wiltshire, south front

26. Lydiard Tregoze, Wiltshire, from the north-east

I was on firmer, rising ground, and ghostly architectural forms loomed out of the snow.

I could just identify a jumble of offices, a stable range, and the church. I was near one Palladian end of the house, and the unfinished parts. There was a gabled projection, and a back door with a bell. The caretaker who came to the door was open-mouthed with incredulity. Having assumed I would come by car, he had put me out of mind because of the storm. He was most friendly, his wife more so, hurrying me to her kitchen. 'Lawks!' she exclaimed, and indeed I *was* a sight, my lovely overcoat black up to the waist with wet mud, my dripping black hat enfolding my ears, my trousers, socks and shoes sodden. Cake and hot tea were pressed upon me and discreetly, with a tinge of embarrassment, the caretaker offered me a set of his old khakis. 'The builders have got a grand brazier in the hall,' he said. 'That'll dry your things off.' I put on an old pair of khaki trousers and a thick Army sweater – the caretaker had served in the Royal Army Service Corps during the war. The fire in the huge iron brazier had died down but the caretaker's wife piled it up with coke, and my clothes were draped around on a circle of chairs. 'Don't worry, dear, these'll dry and we'll take you back to the station in the car when the snow lets up,' she said.

The vicissitudes of my Arctic approach were forgotten in the magical ambience of this house. I gazed around the Palladian hall, as yet pristine in its unrestored state. I recall busts on brackets, one of Viscount Bolingbroke by Rysbrack, dated 1737, surmounting a tall chimney-piece, and a fine coved ceiling, all in a decidedly Kentian style. The southern side of the house had been new-fronted with angle towers, *à la* Wilton; if by Kent, it was Kent in late mood, but I preferred the attribution to Roger Morris. And so I made notes as we progressed slowly through the rooms; the library was Kentian too, but ultimately I came down in favour of Morris. 'Do you want to see the attics and cellars?' the caretaker asked. I paused, then said 'Yes' – an affirmative that would cost me dear. The light was now fading, and there were a few bare bulbs hanging from ceilings. At last we left the house by a back door and went into the church. For monuments 'it exceeds all the churches of this countie', wrote John Aubrey, and truly the presence of 'family' here is suffocating. Their ghosts haunt the place. Heraldic colours and gilding glint in the soft light. Rysbrack was also responsible for the 1748 grey and white marble monument to John, 2nd Viscount St John, who rebuilt Lydiard from 1743 but died before it was completed.

'Well, now for tea, and then we'll take you back.' The snow had lessened, but lay six inches on the ground. Tea was poured, lemon sponge offered and greedily scoffed. I was warm and comfy. My mind kept leaping ahead in time. What would the Borough of Swindon do to the place? I felt deflated by the thought. The atmosphere of the house was so redolent of the St John possession, such a powerful condensation of magic: surely it could never survive? But it has, and although surrounded by a municipal park, the playground for hundreds every weekend, its empty but beautiful rooms remain strongly evocative of the centuries of Bolingbroke occupancy. It is a spellbinding place.

It was time to collect my dry clothes – to my relief, for the rough trousers were itchy around the crotch. As we made our way along a passage there was a sudden reverberating shout of alarm from the caretaker ahead of us as he entered the hall. Smoke was everywhere, and we were met with the smell of scorched and burnt clothes and wood. The brazier, once so dull, was now red and glowing, eagerly consuming overcoat,

trousers and socks, and the backs of two chairs. The mortifica-
tion of Mr and Mrs Caretaker cannot be described. They more
or less prostrated themselves in horror, and insisted on both
coming to the station to see me off. I returned to London, not
in my beautiful new Aquascutum overcoat, now burnt to a
cinder, but in itchy Army issue.

14

The alsatian in the bath

Draycot Cerne, Wiltshire

FROM PEVSNER'S *WILTSHIRE* you would never know that the great house of the Tylney-Longs at Draycot Cerne had ever existed, despite the survival of terraces, substantial stables, and the ancient park so redolent of their long tenure. Longs were here from 1500, and Sir Robert Long's tomb in the church, of 1767, is by Joseph Wilton. Through Sir Robert's marriage in 1735 to Lady Emma Child, daughter of the 1st Earl Tylney, his son Sir James succeeded to the 2nd Earl Tylney's estates in 1784 – hence Tylney-Long; hence, too, the connection with Wanstead and, in the next generation, the cause of the dispersal in a 32-day auction in 1822 of the collections of that great house, and the demolition of the house itself in 1823.

In 1954 I was looking up Tylney in Burke's *Peerage* apropos Wanstead, the first house to become the focus of my amateur interests, trying to find estate papers. Reading of Sir James Long's inheritance, I immediately wanted to visit

Draycot. This was easy: Geoffrey Houghton Brown regularly called on antique dealers John Teed in Bradford-on-Avon and Robin Eden in Pickwick, near Corsham. Before we left London, a call to Chippenham Public Library informed us that Draycot had long been empty, its demolition pending since 1949.

Today the M4 slices through the Draycot estate. Exit 17 was once Tylney-Long land, and when we arrived, we entered the gardens from a lane now obliterated by the access road to that exit. For a mile we passed through Draycot's old hunting park (its hunting lodge is still there, by the M4), then drew in to the rear of the house by the stables. We were confronted by half a dozen cars in various states of undress and dismemberment, attended by a shifty middle-aged garage mechanic in overalls – the so-called caretaker, whose belligerent stare softened when we offered him a pound each for access to the house.

But first we looked at the outsides of the other three fronts. Draycot's architectural history is undocumented, and all the evidence I had was that somewhere on the building was the date 1784, marking the work of Sir James Tylney-Long. One main front possessed a grand tall pedimented centre of five bays, rising up like a pavilion from the wings of five-windowed bays to each side. The other front (?1784) had pairs of canted bays, the third a three-bay pavilion centre with lower wings, but with a tripartite sort of window. Balustraded terraces retained unkempt lawns and shrubberies. Did the family still own the house? I suspect not. We knew that the estates of Wanstead and Draycot had passed to the Earls Cowley who were seated at Draycot in 1913, but that the 4th Earl lived in Nevada.

The man in the greasy overalls was using the rear rooms as a

27. Draycot Cerne, Wiltshire, from the garden

28. Draycot Cerne, Wiltshire, park front

store for car parts. We guessed he was moonlighting, little doubting that cars arrived there in the middle of the night and departed the next morning. The staircase with iron railings looked mid eighteenth-century, but two panelled rooms possessed London-style chimney-pieces of the 1720s. In the so-called Music Room Geoffrey told me about the Watteauesque pictures that had once hung here, recalling that at a sale of the contents he attended he had made a mental note that possibly they resembled the *commedia dell'arte* figures in the under-painting he had found in the Painted Room at his own Winslow Hall. Only later was I able to relate these Draycot paintings to the 'several quaint Watteau-like pictures of the Seasons' panelled on the walls of the Lake House, or Russian Farm, at Wanstead, attributed by Edward Croft-Murray to J.F. Nollekens. I once found an old photograph of these *in situ* in the Lake House, demolished in 1908, but have sadly lost the reference.

Unlike so many destitute houses waiting for the demolition contractors to dismantle them, Draycot had survived relatively unscathed: no windows broken, rooms dry and warm. In retrospect, this was odd, for I had read that Draycot was *in extremis* following military occupation. Upstairs we found handsome plain bedrooms with late eighteenth-century papers still intact, and simple chimney-pieces. Each of the larger attic rooms had a built-in corner cupboard with lead-lined sink and tap.

I wondered about the date of all the fine, austere exterior stone architecture. Was it consistent with what we saw inside? I cannot recall the floor plan, but our sense was of an earlier house enfolded in more recent dress.

There was but one strange and unattractive discovery: opening the door of a bathroom, we quickly withdrew at the sight of the dried-up corpse of an alsatian in the tub. The caretaker said it had been there for two years, and *he* wasn't going to remove it. How did it come to die in the bath, we wondered?

15

Police! Stay where you are!

Wulf Hall, Wiltshire

Having persuaded me to sell him the crown reputedly
embroidered by Catherine of Aragon which Sid bought
me at the Kimbolton Castle sale in 1949, Hector Bruce Bru-
denell Binney, that genial rogue dealer notorious for his reluc-
tance in paying his bills, owed me a favour. He said, 'Go any
time to Wulf Hall. Pick up the key from the Savernake Hotel.
I'll write you a note.' It boded well for a weekend in the
country. All I knew about Wulf Hall was that Jane Seymour
was born there, and it was the fragment of a great Tudor
house on an anciently enparked estate consolidated by
Thomas, Lord Bruce, at nearby Tottenham Park in the early
eighteenth century. Hector's mother was a daughter of the 5th
Marquess of Ailesbury, the descendant of that Lord Bruce. It
was a misty November in 1954 and in that pre-Beeching era
steam trains stopped at Savernake, so I did too. But why did
the hotel manager seem surprised? Why suggest that there
might not be water or electricity, and that I should buy tinned

food and candles from the village shop? It was not long before I discovered: in expressing his own alarm, the shopkeeper said he couldn't recollect anyone staying at the house since 1947.

Hector's instructions, to one who never drives, were to 'walk the canal tow-path to the first bridge, turn right, and the house is on the hill'. It was, but totally hidden in a grove of trees, and brambled-in to a height of six feet. An iron gate with piers should have framed the Henry Flitcroft wing, so-called because Wulf Hall was made habitable for use while Flitcroft and Lord Burlington were rebuilding Tottenham Park in 1720, but I could only just spy the front above the brambles.

First the gate had to be forced, then scratches and stings endured in order to approach a white wooden porch leaning precariously to one side. It leaned even more when the door fell open and outwards, to reveal a surreal ensemble of a white bust on a pedestal, a rusted twelve-bore gun, a pile of mildewed books, and a huge wasps' nest that sent me into hasty retreat. (I later wondered whether the gun was the same one used by Hector when he shot Lord Ailesbury's pet deer by mistake. He had been given grudging permission to go shooting on the estate. Hardly had he left the gardens when he saw this deer approaching, and gleefully shot it in triumph. Alas, it had a collar around its neck.) In any case, the key did not fit the inner door. Ten minutes later a door in the Tudor wing at the back yielded to my persuasions, opening on a kitchen out of which fled many cats, followed by even more kittens.

Even after forty years – how to describe the interior, stuffed with the left-overs from Tottenham Park? Cabinets on stands, busts, chairs with rotten covers, veneers curling from tables and chests, Seymour and Bruce portraits and Gaspardeseque landscapes invisible for mildew, curtains torn, an overall layering of dust and cobwebs, and dirty windows inducing gloom.

As predicted, there was no water or electricity. I had to make a plan, a base for myself in this cold, spooky house.

A pair of ormolu candelabra was set on a French *bureau-plat* in a vestibule next to a bedroom with a Biedermeier swan bed. Downstairs, a door was forced, revealing a library in chaos. There was a chimney-piece at one end, French windows to one side, and down the centre temporary wooden stacks, from which books had fallen or been thrown across the room, discards from the great Ailesbury book sale at Tottenham in 1919. I remember a huge volume of Callot etchings bound in embellished green calf, Robert Boyle's copy of Switzer's *Ichnographica Rustica*, and Cundy's drawings for the further rebuilding of Tottenham in 1825. Here would be my HQ, as I termed it. So a comfortable chair was arranged, and with some apprehension I lit a fire in the grate – which was followed by much flapping of wings.

Curiosity demanded a full examination of cupboards and drawers. In one were vintage gramophone records, all of Caruso; a Flemish cabinet was stuffed with jewellery, incredibly not all junk or paste; a chest contained a mass of early fringes and tassels and pieces of embroidery; and a box was full of identified samples of Roman marbles. In retrospect, I wonder whether, if I had looked further, I would have found the jewel-encrusted Order of the Garter given in trust to Thomas Bruce when James II fled the country? It was mistakenly given by Lord Ailesbury to Hector to use for his amateur theatricals, and when he tried later to sell it at Sotheby's, Queen Elizabeth said, 'No, that must be returned to me.' Poor Hector.

Night cast its fearful shadows, setting my imagination racing. I took one candelabrum into the library, opened a tin of baked beans and a bottle of Tizer, and drew a chair up to the fire. I distinctly remember turning the pages of a volume of engravings by Gribelin; suddenly, warm contentment was turned to terror – there at the French window was pressed a white face, and a leaning hand. I leapt up, the candles went flying, all was thrown into darkness except for the light of the fire. A voice bellowed: 'Police! Stay where you are!' Shaking, I let the law in, gave a breathless explanation and displayed Hector's letter – but did not point out that the end of the man's nose was covered in black smears. He apologised and said he was there quite by chance; Hector had asked the police to keep an eye on the house, but he didn't pass by very often. He thought Hector had been there once, maybe twice.

All this took a few minutes. The law departed, and with dry mouth I went to the kitchen for more Tizer, only to see a gloved hand appearing through a broken window, trying the catch. It was another policeman, who had taken the house from the rear, but of course, not realising at first that this was a second arm of the law, I asked with some annoyance what on earth he wanted *now*. However, even in the failing light I could see no dirtied nose, and deduced another bobby. More explanations had to be given, then law number one arrived on the scene. It was all too much. I retreated to the swan bed, to listen to Caruso on one of those wind-up gramophones with a large horn and needles that need constant changing.

A night full of improbable dreams was followed by a sudden dawn that awakened me with a 'tap, tap, tap' on the single window in this white-panelled room. 'Not again,' I thought. Should I pretend not to be there? Should I rush the door? Should I raise my head and face my fate? I did the last, to see a magpie, who continued to tap until I left the room. I decided then and there to retrace my steps along the towpath, and wait for the fragrant steam-train to Reading.

But first I made a quick exploration of the overgrown

garden. I found a decayed greenhouse with bunches of unpicked grapes, a Gothic arbour collapsed to the ground, and a marble classical capital I longed to pinch. When I looked up at the wing adjacent to Flitcroft's front, my eyes lighted upon a pair of windows with tasselled blinds and faded curtains. I stared, and thought, and made a calculation about the plan of the house. This was my Biedermeier bedroom, which had only one window, and that on the other front! I rushed upstairs, wondering if it was all a dream. It was not: the late nineteenth-century panelling had been put straight across the existing windows and all their fittings.

'Rather you than me,' said the hotel manager, and as a reward for my courage gave me a free lunch. Only once did I return to Wulf Hall, long after Hector's Order of the Garter had been taken away. Alas, the place had been emptied and the garden tidied; the magic was gone. I met Hector only once again, when Eileen and I were browsing in Hall's bookshop in Tunbridge Wells. From behind a bookcase rose Hector's head (the spitting image of Sir John Seymour's effigy in Great Bedwyn church) to give me greeting. According to Rupert Gunnis, he was up to no good as the self-appointed guardian of Chiddingstone Castle, where he was under suspicion of nicking Stuart and Jacobite relics, while the owner, Denys Bower, was languishing in one of Her Majesty's holiday camps.

16

Snorting, needling, and murky liaisons

Belvedere, Kent

I N A LETTER to Rupert Gunnis in 1954 I enclosed a snap of a fragment of a Roman altar bought by Geoffrey Houghton Brown from an antique shop in Gravesend. This had reputedly been dug up from the garden at Ingress Abbey, Greenhithe, just up the Thames. Colvin's *Dictionary* informed me that at Ingress John Calcraft had housed a collection of Roman altars in a temple designed by Sir William Chambers; to which I added the information from R. Dodsley's *London and its Environs* (1761) that Ingress had been the seat of the 2nd Earl of Bessborough, who of course was a great collector of antique marbles; in his grief at the death of his wife in January 1760 he sold Ingress, and commissioned Chambers to build him a villa at Roehampton. Both owners of course figured in the biography of Chambers I was later to write, so this earlier interest in Ingress seems prophetic.

Not for the first time, I took a train to Greenhithe. This was well-known territory to me, since like many an archaeologist, pseudo or otherwise, I had paid homage at nearby Swanscombe, the site of prehistoric Swanscombe Man, found in one of the many gravel-workings thereabouts. At Ingress were no bones, but an Elizabethan-style villa of the 1830s built by Charles Moreing for James Harmer and now occupied by HMS *Worcester*, a Naval Training College. It did not capture my imagination, but the site and garden did. Lord Bessborough's had been a scenic choice, made even more picturesque by the passing water traffic.

When laying my plans I had been tempted to return to Greenhithe from Ingress and continue on down-river to Milton, where I could have crossed the Thames to Tilbury to see Tilbury Fort; but in turning the pages of Dodsley I was drawn to his engraving of Sir Sampson Gideon's house at Belvedere. I noticed a station of this name up-river from Greenhithe, next to Erith, and Howard Colvin again came to my aid with information about the rebuilding of the house in about 1775 for Gideon, then Lord Eardley, by James Stuart. It was all too much. What was I to expect?

I suppose in those days there *were* xerox machines, but not in Collin and Winslow. As I was making a rough sketch from Dodsley, it seemed to me that the bones of the house were of earlier vintage, maybe of the Lord Baltimore who died there in 1751, and that a Great Room had been added to one side. Leaving Belvedere station I climbed a hill to its summit, then turned off to find gate piers and a drive still surrounded by parkland. The gate was chained; I was becoming used to this, and saw that the wire fence to one side, bent down, bore the familiar signs of constant illegal access.

A huge, towering house confronted me, evoking comparison to a barracks by virtue of its plain stock-brick construction. I was looking at the unadorned entrance front to the south, with outer canted bays set under Diocletian attic windows and in the centre a stone porch–portico. What really took my eye was the Great Room attached to one side, with a magnificent Palladian window–door in ashlar and rusticated stone. I later attributed this to Isaac Ware, but Richard Garnier (whom I affectionately call Tick Tock Taylor, since he is an expert on both Sir Robert Taylor and clocks) believes it to be Taylor's, on the grounds of its rococo interior. I could see that James Stuart must have turned the whole house round, his new entrance front facing south, the earlier one west.

Hardly had I begun my examination when a harridan emerged from a hidden corner as if charging onto a battlefield, except that she had no bayonet. I am no misogynist, but even today find female minders of houses less amenable than male to flattery or bribes. 'I'm a Gideon,' I lied, 'a descendant of Eardley Gideon who emigrated to Canada in the last century. I was told I should come here, as the house is going to be demolished.' My deception cost me five shillings, but the harridan led me to the side door from which she had charged and, happily, left me to my own devices.

A confession to shock many: in those days, when I was not yet a proper architectural historian, I often missed much of significance. I bitterly regret this in the case of Belvedere particularly, as I seem to be the only historian (or quasi-historian) who ever got inside. That an earlier house had been retained as the core was obvious, and I found a late Palladian room and a white marble chimney-piece of similar mid-century date. There was also a dining room with a screen of Corinthian columns, possibly early. Everywhere – my memory is clear on this point – were splendid cast-iron coke stoves set in front of handsome, mostly Stuart, chimney-

29. Belvedere, Kent, south entrance front

30. Belvedere, Kent, Stuart chimney-piece and coke stove

pieces, the stoves imported when the house was a school or college. I progressed across the south front, and entered the Great Room. What I remember of this must be conflated with what I have seen since in the few interior photographs that have survived. I was in a decidedly rococo room, with a rich plasterwork cove and doors in French rococo taste. For this reason, in an article in *Connoisseur* in 1961, I wrote that I thought the room to have been Lord Baltimore's, equating its French decoration with his French interiors at Woodcote Park: his originally was the set of paintings of the *commedia dell'arte* signed by Andien de Clermont in 1742, then in the collection of a customer of Geoffrey's who had acquired them from Belvedere. This was a convenient pointer to the date of Baltimore's interior decorations, and I made the observation that Clermont had also painted for him at Woodcote.

I moved on to the rooms facing the river – and gasped! The house was built precipitously on a slope, its basement dropping below ground level as a retaining elevation to cellars, but from each side of the house huge wings, at their outer limits two storeys high, extended outwards, making a U-shaped enclosure open to the river. It was spectacular, if odd, evoking something Italianate, an echo of Roman terrace works. I unbolted the central door and found myself above garden stairs with the vast Palladian window–door behind me. Below-stairs one wing was for kitchens, the other was tantalisingly locked. Beneath the central stairs were Roman vaulted rooms, of antique derivation, maybe intended as a columbarium. The view back to the house from the lower garden was extraordinary. Somehow I felt ancient Rome had featured in its inspiration. It was a tragedy that this was never documented in photographs.

I have not commented that the weather was stormy. Rain belted down, and I hurried back into a darkened house. There was an elegant Stuart library, many more Stuart chimney-pieces and rooms with Stuart trim. The real find was upstairs, where a room on the south front was hung with Georgian chinoiserie papers, mounted on canvas and battened to the walls, but defaced by someone who had gone round poking a finger in as many places as possible. Many pokes were high up. How did they achieve this, unless they were giants? I thought then of a story Geoffrey had told me, of a house requisitioned in 1941. It had a rare painted paper with peacock decoration, which the owner had efficiently boarded up before his temporary exile. When he returned in 1946 he took the seemingly untampered-with boards down, to find to his horror that all the peacocks' eyes had been carefully cut out. Fifteen years later, an envelope arrived with an American postmark, and out of it fell all the eyes, with a small piece of paper on which was written 'So sorry!'

I bade farewell to the harridan, ruminating that I had probably paid her too much; but it had been worth it. The rain had ceased, and on the wooded headland overlooking the Thames I found a neo-classical pedestal and a ruined temple. I returned with Rupert Gunnis in 1958 or 1959, when the place was efficiently boarded-up and inaccessible. It was demolished a few years later. Crowthers of the North End Road bought some chimney-pieces, but I never discovered who bought the lovely Stuart bookcases. I returned again in 1996 with Eileen, Tim and Todd. We gave up any attempt to locate the site precisely, as it was now an unattractive place blitzed by shoddy 1950s development. As for the wooded headland, so nasty was its miasma that we shuddered, declining to see if the pedestal or temple were still there. We passed a broken-down piece of wall, all that remained *in situ* of poor Belvedere. As we left by the old approach lane, we saw a huddle of men conspiring behind bushes: the place was given over to snorting, needling, and murky liaisons.

17

Getting the better of the Rothschild agent

The Winchendon Pavilion, Buckinghamshire

IN 1954 OR 1955, whenever we went shopping in Aylesbury from Winslow Hall, it was a dereliction of duty not to visit Weatherhead's bookshop: country bookshops in those happy days were treasure-troves. (Nowadays, for Weatherhead, read Waterstones.) There I bought a copy of George Lipscombe's *History and Antiquities of the County of Buckingham*. Browsing through it later at Winslow, I was intrigued by a description of the Marquess of Wharton's Winchendon House at Upper Winchendon. What was there now? Lacking Pevsner's *Buckinghamshire*, I could only refer to the map, on which I spied the park of Waddesdon, contiguous to Eythrope to the south, divided from it only by a lane. What remained of the Wharton house was on this lane, near Upper Winchendon church. Philip, Lord Wharton (1613–96), the 4th Baron, 'loved splendour', wrote Lipscombe, providing tantalising hints as to the Whartons' comparably great gardens at Wooburn on the Thames. In his *Dictionary* of 1954 Colvin referred to Eythrope under Isaac Ware ('stables and garden buildings for Sir William Stanhope, *c.* 1750') and also under Thomas Harris (the 'handsome new front' seen by Dr Pococke, *c.* 1751). I later found that the three estates of Waddesden, Eythrope and Winchendon had been amalgamated in the nineteenth century as Rothschild territory, but for the present I had two objects in mind: to visit Miss Dorothy Harris, who possessed in her house at Wing annotated copies of Thomas Harris's books; and to visit Winchendon to elucidate Lipscombe's reference to the Marquess of Wharton's maze – or, as it is described in accounts of Wharton's stud, his 'wilderness'. Lipscombe mentioned the rectilinear divisions and terraces then traceable, and located the wilderness to the east of the house. What particularly took my eye, however, was his description of a 'small turreted brick building' built by Lord Wharton 'for the residence of a favourite lady . . . Its situation though solitary, commanded a remarkably fine view, embracing the race course in Quainton meadow, and the adjacent fields, about two miles distant.' I felt a tingle. Was it still there? The Ordnance Survey map showed a green strip against the lane, and to one side a tiny black dot indicating some sort of building.

At Winslow, Geoffrey Houghton Brown warned me about the Waddesden agent who lived in what survived of the Wharton great house: he was by reputation difficult and obstructive, erecting 'Keep Out' notices around the gardens, and actively patrolling them. Geoffrey had bought a beautifully-painted heraldic hatchment of one Lord Wharton, but his offer of it to the agent (a military man) elicited terse and uncomplimentary remarks about dealers, and over-priced wares. Undeterred by all this, I charted out an indirect approach, via Eythrope. It was my intention to spy out the park, in the hope that something might survive of the Stanhope house and Isaac Ware's temples

31. Winchendon House, Buckinghamshire, the Pavilion

– avoiding, of course, Mrs de Rothschild, who then lived in the nineteenth-century house at Eythrope.

A hidden entry into Eythrope Park took me to a lake off the river Thame, where I found a partly-ruined Palladian bridge. Years later, with the aid of Howard Colvin's article 'Eythrope House and its Demolition in 1810–11' (1964) and my own copy of Ware's *Complete Body of Architecture* (1756), I found an engraving of this bridge, and lamented that Ware's two fine Palladian temples were no more. This parkland walk brought me to the fringe of the old gardens at Winchendon, flanking the lane. Here I nipped across and dived into the wood, finding myself on the Waddesden side of Winchendon, with views towards Quainton as described by Lipscombe. I was in the old 'wilderness', and if I could remain unseen, I would defeat the agent yet.

Then my heart gave a jerk: there, in an angle where wood

and hedge joined, was the pavilion. I crept quietly along the edge of the wood and assaulted the pavilion from the rear. It was of brick, the main body with a higher centre and lower wings, all its windows arcuated or round-headed, a watered-down version of Sir John Vanbrugh's style. With these Vanbrughian characteristics in mind, I imagined it to have been built by Thomas Harris, whose designs for the Prison and County Hall in Aylesbury were vetted by Vanbrugh in 1720. However, the agent's house was near, so danger threatened from that direction.

The pavilion was obviously abandoned. First I peered through the windows, to gasp at empty panelled rooms with coved ceilings and bolection moulded chimney-pieces. How I yearned to get in. I tried the door – and it just opened! What met my eyes was a perfectly preserved interior, surely of the time of Thomas, the 5th Baron, who was Earl of Wharton in 1706 and Marquess in 1715, the year he died – but only just; or, if by Harris, then old-fashioned. A stair of twisted balusters opened off a vestibule. In every room the bolections were marbled, and the upper room was completely panelled and floored with inlaid woods. Two chimney-pieces were tucked into corners. All the glazing was of that old, wobbly greenish glass. Some years later, I was able to associate its interior with that of Swansgrove at Badminton. Back at Winslow, Geoffrey could not believe my tale. Determined to see the place, he foolishly drove up the drive to ask formal permission, and was sent packing by the agent, shouting and gesticulating: 'Can't you read the "Private" and "No Entry" notices?'

There is a dreadful conclusion to this tale. In 1978 I was in correspondence with the late Robert Bevan, who owned a painting of Winchendon showing elaborate parterres and topiary screens and alleys. This I identified as probably by Peter

Tillemans and related it to drawings by Tillemans owned by Mr Paul Mellon. I then concluded that the gardens had been laid out by Thomas, the 5th Baron, who inherited in 1696, and were possibly by the same man who made the topiary gardens at nearby Hartwell House. Once more my interest in the secret pavilion was aroused, but somehow I never returned there. Quite recently, lunching with Christopher Gibbs and Jacob Rothschild at Eythrope, we determined to seek out the pavilion that had so enchanted me. Christopher and I plodded over ploughed fields, searching in vain. Indeed, I was in the dog-house – both he and Jacob believed I had been dreaming. My reputation was salvaged when we made enquiry at a nearby cottage, where a rustic youth recollected a pavilion that had been demolished by the agent 'many years ago'. Beastly agent!

An odd postscript to this story concerns Thomas Harris. Sometime in the late 1960s I had a telephone call from my friends David Style and Jonathan Vickers. In Burford that day they had called upon Roger Warner, that best of country antique dealers. He was away, but lying on his desk was a handsome thick folio bound in red calf with (what first caught their eyes) the inscription in gilt, 'T. Harris'. It contained his designs, with engravings and water-colour views. I should telephone Roger. With mounting excitement I did so, to be deflated by his denial of ever having had such a volume. I rang Jonathan and David, who assured me they *had* seen it there. Years later I quizzed them again, and they still vigorously denied my accusation that it was all a joke.

18

A day in Hampshire but not Hinton Ampner

Warnford Park – The Grange – Stratton Park –
Kempshott House

I
N APRIL 1956 Felix Harbord was offered a Regency chimney-piece by a dealer in Alton, Hampshire. It was from Warnford Park, by rumour soon to be demolished, and the dealer also had some furniture from the house, whose interiors were being picked over. Felix invited Geoffrey Houghton Brown to meet him in Alton. Geoffrey's plan was to see the dealer, go on to Warnford, then on again to Ralph Dutton's at nearby Hinton Ampner to spend the weekend. Prosser's lithograph of Warnford in his *Hampshire* showed a plain house built mostly by the Lords Clanricarde, and added to after 1824 by William Abbott, a squire from Northamptonshire who may have used his local architect, John Leachman, for improvements.

We met in Alton, and drove in two cars to Warnford Park, turning in through Leachman's entrance arch of the stables. Partial demolition had begun: men were working on the staircase and columned hall, chimney ornaments were piled in the approach yard, and a labourer in bright red overalls was prising up an inlaid patterned floor in the Ionic-columned dining room. There was a hurried consultation between Felix and Mr Red Overalls, no doubt involving the passing of notes, and the Regency floor was his. It was very difficult to elucidate the architectural history of the house. It was entirely stuccoed, but the entrance front with its pilastered attic storey had Palladian proportions. Only later was I able to tentatively associate this with Matthew Brettingham, who had made designs for the 11th Earl of Clanricarde in 1754, basing my theory on the evidence of a broken Palladian chimney-piece of decidedly Brettingham vintage on the lawn. We were told the estate had been sold in 1934, and the house requisitioned from a Mr R.P. Chester in 1940. First occupied by the Lancashire Fusiliers, then by Combined Operations prior to D-Day, the ensuing saga was the familiar one of ill-treatment and lack of maintenance. The house was shut up in despair in 1946, and dry rot and vandals took their toll.

The park was attractively watered by the river Meon, forming a large lake. Pevsner's *Hampshire* does not tell us whether the grandly-walled kitchen garden is still there. Surely it must be? If this great Clanricarde seat has been forgotten, medieval historians have worked to death the ruins of King John's Lodge on the approach to the Clanricarde house, an early thirteenth-century hall house built by Adam de Port, who held Warnford until his death in 1213. We passed it by, more pleased to find in the park the Gothick House, a charming flint and stone summer pavilion with a grotto tunnel, one of Clanricarde's follies.

We then moved on to Hinton Ampner. I had met Ralph Dutton once at Thurloe Square, and yearned to see his house with its resplendent collection. Many of the art works and

32. Warnford Park, Hampshire, entrance front in demolition, April 1956

33. Stratton Park, Hampshire, the stair-hall, 1951

34. Stratton Park, Hampshire, entrance front

35. The Grange, Hampshire,
from the south-east, September 1972

36. Kempshott House, Hampshire, garden front, 1962

decorative objects that furnished it came from Geoffrey. I had hoped to be invited in, but alas! we parted at the house, and Geoffrey sent me back with Felix. (I was very fond of Felix with his ferrety quizzical face and was attracted by his flair as a decorator. He lacked John Fowler's *gravitas*; for him decorating was fun and, unlike John, he thirsted for the hunt involved in tracking antique spoils. He possessed a wondrous facility for keeping incomplete accounts.) There were compensations and treats in store, however. We had lunch at The Grange with old Mr Wallach, whom I had met only recently with Derek Sherborn. He was still bitter that his offer of the house and contents to the government had been rejected in the 1930s. At that time few people were familiar with his distinguished collection of Old Masters, including four landscapes by Goya. Poor Wallach: when war was declared his friends assured him that as his house was set so prominently Greek-like on its hill, it would certainly be bombed. More than a hundred Old Masters were therefore sent into store in a warehouse in Southampton − and it was this the Luftwaffe bombed. The house was forlorn: aged and infirm, Mr Wallach simply couldn't cope. He had retreated to a few small rooms in a connecting wing with all that remained of his once-famous collection of Old Masters. How could we have suspected that when it was sold to the Barings after Wallach's death, they would threaten to blow it up, by coincidence in 1972, the very year of the great 'Age of Neo-Classicism' exhibition at the Royal Academy of Arts, in which it featured prominently? We went on to Herriard Park to have tea with the Jervoises, who even then were moaning about the inconveniences of their baroque house, which they finally demolished in 1965. They used John James's architectural model as a dolls' house.

The real treat was Stratton Park, a few miles on. Yet again, the Barings' demolition contractors would soon be at work. Until 1803 Stratton had been a grand Palladian house, designed in 1731 for the 3rd Duke of Bedford by John Sanderson. Protective of Woburn, the 4th Duke partly dismantled Stratton, and it was the one remaining wing of this reduced house that Sir Francis Baring purchased in 1800, employing John Dance the Younger to rebuild, adding its powerful Greek portico, and to decorate all the rooms. Felix had a persuasive way with custodians and caretakers, no doubt aided by folding money changing hands. It was a touch of the cap, and 'Door's open, sir.'

Even today, one mutters and wonders 'How could they?' What a monstrous decision to demolish everything of Stratton except the portico. Although the house had deteriorated through war misuse, its condition was not severe. The Barings simply preferred the modern house built here in 1963 to the Frenchified elegance of Dance's interiors. We were stunned by the neo-Greek entrance hall and staircase and, walking through Dance's rooms, caught our breath at the Gallic elegance of his trim, noticing *en route* one of Sanderson's Palladian chimney-pieces with overmantel. We were even more excited by a white marble chimney-piece, attributed by Prosser in his *Hampshire* to Canova. (I have Prosser by me now, and marvel at his descriptions of the rich art collections.) As we left, Felix was muttering about how to get his hands on that Canova chimney-piece. Had he managed to, he would eventually have discovered that Canova never designed chimney-pieces, and that this exquisite work was by the sculptor John de Vaere.

We left by way of the London Lodge, one of Dance's mongrel combinations of classical lodge and Gothic arch, onto the main road for Basingstoke. With the Ordnance Survey map at hand I noticed Kempshott House, remembering it from

Prosser. I later read that in 1773 Philip Dehany demolished an earlier house and built a 'large mansion, of plain exterior, but handsome and commodious within', sold to John Morley in 1787, and sold again by auction in 1788 to John Crosse Crooke, who was then renting Stratton Park. Poor Crooke! In 1789 he was leant on by George, Prince of Wales, and obliged to lease Kempshott out for several years for the Prince's hunting and shooting.

We found a brooding house, dark and gloomy, its stucco crumbling, deserted, abandoned to agricultural use. According to Prosser, Edward Walter Blunt employed Sampson Kempthorne in 1832 for remodelling work, which explained the late Italianate additions. There were potatoes inside, and bales of hay, and an end wall had been broken open at ground floor level to shelter a tractor. One fine room remained, reasonably attributable to Henry Holland. The chimney-piece had gone, and may well have been the very one incorporated by Robersons the Knightsbridge dealers into the 'Kempshott Park Room' they installed in the late 1920s at the St Louis Museum of Art. I first discovered this room in 1962, and was able to associate it with the alterations made by Holland for the Prince Regent (at the same time, I discovered his exterior designs for Kempshott in the Royal Library); with excitement, I published it. Only later did I discover the room for what it was, a spoof made up from several houses and some decorator's inventions, and so came to write about the 'Room that never was'. Robersons' plunder clearly indicated that the house was being dismantled in the 1920s, when I suspect it was an abandoned casualty of the First World War.

19

A welcome bout of 'flu

Fairford Park, Gloucestershire

SHORTLY BEFORE DOING my National Service in 1949 I stayed at the Duntisbourne Abbots youth hostel – not a dole-induced stop, for once, but in order to walk in the wooded valley of the river Frome, north of Stroud's Golden Valley. I passed by Daneway, ignorant of Oliver Hill and Cotswold Arts and Crafts, and have no memory of how I ended up at Tetbury – possibly it was through a lift on the Stroud road. I am embarrassed that whereas Tetbury is a town I now know well, my only recollection of it in 1949 is of the railway station. Here I was on familiar ground, for the Tetbury to Kemble branch line of the Great Western Railway had similar rolling stock to the branch line of my childhood, from Uxbridge via Cowley to West Drayton. The livery was brown and yellow, and even the engine was the same: an 0-4-02. At Tetbury a deferential porter told me of a connection from Kemble to Cirencester, stopping at Culkerton and Rodmarton. Murray's *Handbook*, fortified by Beckinsale's *Companion into Gloucester-*

shire and The Cotswolds, determined my destination from
Cirencester: I would take a bus to Fairford, attracted there by
Murray's description of the famous stained glass in the church.
Sid knew Fairford well: I was jealous because he had stayed in
the Bull Hotel and fished the river Coln. I reckoned I would
just make the Charney Bassett youth hostel that night. My
memory of the Fairford glass has of course been enriched and
amplified by many subsequent visits to that church over the
past twenty-five years. I cannot now say whether in 1949 I
noticed the tomb of Valentine Strong, who died in 1662; if I
did, I would not have associated him with the building of
adjacent Fairford Park, nor would I have made the connection
even when I returned to Fairford in 1955.

On this second visit I was with Felix Harbord. Geoffrey
Houghton Brown and Felix had intended to visit Gavin Faringdon at Faringdon Park, but Geoffrey had 'flu, so Felix
chose me as his stand-in. When we arrived we found as guests
Gerald Berners and Robert Heber-Percy, a couple whom
Felix later described as 'wickedees'. In the hall I had my first
introduction to the furniture of Thomas Hope, for Gavin possessed Hope's Egyptian suite from his house in Duchess Street.
Later at lunch the fashion for Regency Revival was discussed,
and Geoffrey, his friend and fellow antique dealer Ronald
Fleming, and the collector, connoisseur and writer of books
published by Batsfords, Ralph Dutton of Hinton Ampner,
were singled out as pioneering enthusiasts for Regency furniture in the 1930s. Felix wanted to move on to visit an antique
dealer in Fairford and one in Lechlade. I would willingly have
stayed at Faringdon, but the Lechlade dealer's comment that
Fairford Park was being demolished that very week brought a
gleam to the eyes of us both.

We made a detour for a glimpse of Lord St Aldwyn's

Williamstrip Park, where I think Felix had some decorating job in view, and from Quenington we crossed the same Coln that we would meet again at Fairford. As we approached the park, we first saw an obelisk in the distance, then came to the ubiquitous park wall, but a huge hutted camp laid out in an aisled grid was unexpected. At the house we were told this had been the American hospital serving the major RAF and USAF bombing station nearby, evoking thoughts of wounded airmen returning from bombing raids. The camp was subsequently a Polish resettlement hostel. Along the drive from near the church to the house were empty Nissen huts, a memorial of the army's occupation of the house.

Indeed, as the Lechlade dealer had warned, demolition was in progress, although as it was a Saturday work had been halted for the weekend. I recall that we paused, undecided whether to drive directly into the stable courtyard where we had glimpsed a foreman's caravan. We were mesmerised by the scene that met our eyes. Felix said the house was like a martyr who had had his tongue torn out, then his eyes pierced, before being half-strangled prior to burning at the stake. Given the all-clear by the foreman, we clambered through and around the dying house. The roof was off, the interiors were gutted, and the lovely Restoration doorway with its curly scrolled pediment joined to the window above was about to be removed. The Gibbsian façade stood precariously, without support at the back. Lying on the lawn were piles of Restoration panelling, some marbelised woodwork, and dismantled Soanic chimney-pieces. At the rear a bonfire burned acridly.

Nicholas Kingsley, the architectural historian of the county, tells the story of the house: of Valentine and Thomas Strong in 1661 building a miniature Coleshill set in formal gardens

37. Fairford Park,
Gloucestershire, north front
in demolition, 1951

38. Fairford Park,
Gloucestershire,
Soanic chimney-pieces, 1955

39. Fairford Park, Gloucestershire,
the Orangery before removal, 1962

for Andrew Barker – all engraved by Jan Kip for Sir Robert Atkyns's *Glostershire* in 1712. This was followed by a refronting for James Lambe in the 1740s, with Gibbsian-style rusticated windows; finally, work by Sir John Soane in 1789 was concurrent with a new landscaping of the old formal gardens by William Eames.

We were offered mugs of tea by the foreman, and learned that the Ernest Cook Trust had bought the house and 2,400 acres from the executors of the Raymond Barkers in 1945. I later read that the estate had been rejected by the National Trust in 1948, following which the house and park had been vested in an educational charity. There had been a disputatious sale to the County Council in 1955 with no provision to incorporate the house into the fabric of the new secondary school built in 1962 by R.F. Fairhurst, who seems to have been an expert in building fire and police stations.

And so down came Fairford Park in that cursed year of 1955, one of those demolitions that took place 'one every two and a half days'. We walked into the kitchen garden adjacent to the stable yard, and beyond it into a woodland that might once have been a late seventeenth-century wilderness. Here was a Doric orangery or greenhouse, now I believe attributed to Sir John Soane, that had been allowed to fall into ruin during the war years. Ornamented with Coade stone plaques, this little masterpiece of garden architecture was taken into care by The National Trust: instead of re-erecting it on one of its properties, the Trust gave it away to Sledmere House, where it has remained dismantled – a second scandal hovering over poor Fairford. I know we inspected a boat-house nearby, but have no recollection if it was the same as the one in the form of a miniature Palladian bridge to be seen in a photograph taken in 1905 and published in *Fairford and Lechlade in Old*

Photographs (1987). I have no recollection of then seeing the Doric Temple, but have since sat in it many times with David and Rosemary Verey, who had it removed to their garden at Barnsley House. There were once urns, cascades and grottoes ornamenting the grounds of Fairford, but the formal long canal had been broadened into a sylvan stretch of water. As Felix and I walked around the lake, the trout were rising with tempting plops. I yearned for my rod, and once again felt envious of Sid's piscatorial triumphs on this very Coln.

20

The King's Champion of England

Scrivelsby Court, Lincolnshire

ALTHOUGH OF GREAT antiquity, the family of Dymoke of Scrivelsby Court in Lincolnshire were never ennobled, but remained the archetype of the English squire. From the time of the Conquest, the senior Dymoke of the family was chosen as the Grand Champion of England, the commoner who would hammer at the door of Westminster Hall at each coronation to uphold the right of the new sovereign against all comers. It is not clear if there were ever any challenges, or what might have happened to Squire Dymoke if there had been. I have read that Henry Dymoke, the last King's Champion, at the Coronation of George IV in 1820, had to borrow a well-trained horse from Astley's Circus, for fear he would otherwise fall off.

It was said that the old Scrivelsby Court had been destroyed by fire in the early nineteenth century, and replaced by a Picturesque, Tudor-style house, and this was reiterated by my friend Henry Thorold in his excellent *Lincolnshire* (1965). An opportunity for me to see what was there presented itself in

1955, when Geoffrey Houghton Brown and I drove from Winslow to visit one of his favourite antique dealers in Grantham. Having been a friend of Lord Curzon's architect, A.S.G. Butler, Geoffrey wanted to see Tattershall Castle, so we decided to call there on the way to Scrivelsby, and return via Spalding, for tea, to Winslow.

As we came to the lodge of Scrivelsby we spied the church standing alone in a field some way off, set against a wood, and decided to eat our picnic in the churchyard. We imagined the interior of the church would be crammed with an accumulation of funerary monuments to a family so long established in this ancient place, but alas! we found nothing special, only a few simple wall monuments and tablets, and an effigy. It seemed that the Dymokes had returned from their coronation appearances to their habitual obscurity without being infected by any desire for grandiose display. We ruminated on the generation after generation of forgotten Dymokes carried across the road from the big house to their burial place. Then we returned to the lodge.

Here the Dymokes' role as King's Champion was romantically symbolised by the Lion Gate, an arch supporting a proud stone Lion of England. When I was working on Pevsner's *Lincolnshire* later, I concluded that this gate had been designed by C.J. Carter in 1833. I also discovered that Humphry Repton had laid out the park in 1791, and that the octagonal lodge by the gate was by him. At the lodge we were questioned by a caretaker, who then let us proceed to the house. Expecting something of early Victorian date – the original having been 'destroyed by fire' – we were thunderstruck by what we saw: in front of us was the gatehouse range, brick and more or less fourteenth-century, altered in 1574, and again in the eighteenth century by Georgian Dymokes. Behind it across the courtyard

40. Scrivelsby Court, Lincolnshire, from the north-east, 1956

stood the south range, which may well have been C.J. Carter's work following the reputed fire, but was essentially only a mending of the court range of a great and ancient medieval house, as was apparent when viewed from the rear.

The ruin that met our eyes can hardly be believed. Its condition was due to the neglect of reclusive Dymokes, rather than to the infantry regiments who surrounded the house during the war. Even in 1938 the Society for the Protection of Ancient Buildings complained of its decay, when it was occupied by the old and eccentric Frank Scaman Dymoke. It was in such a derelict state when we saw it that not only were we in danger of falling through the floors, but it seemed that the house might just collapse upon us. We had to avoid holes by tiptoeing gingerly across beams over yawning spaces, we could see daylight up above, and although neither of us was an enthusiast for medieval crucks and braces, we both marvelled at the exposure of its ancient construction. It was possible to ascend but one stair, and in the only accessible room (where the floors had not dropped into the room below) were fragments of mural painting on plaster. Geoffrey prised off a lump depicting the head of a medieval woman. The concentration of antiquity was uncanny, of the sort that Horace Walpole called the 'True Rust of the Barons' Wars', as confirmation of feudal age. Behind the site of what I supposed was a screens passage the fallen plaster had exposed a late-Norman arch. Few rallied to Scrivelsby's distress, and it had disappeared by the time I came this way again in 1959, when all I could discern were partially-watered moats and the turf outlines of formal gardens within this Reptonian park with its herds of deer.

Spalding was very different, with its Dutch canals and red-brick architecture. Only later did I associate this town and its Ayscoughfee Hall with Maurice Johnson, who founded the Spalding Gentlemen's Society in 1710 and laid out the formal topiary garden, the amazing topiary now overgrown and of gigantic size, like surreal floats swaying in the wind.

21

Clock trouble, or 'Old Testicle'

Oving House, Buckinghamshire

I N 1954 I visited Winslow Hall, Buckinghamshire, for the first time. This tall beautifully austere red brick house dominating the village is documented as having been built by Sir Christopher Wren in 1699 for William Lowndes, Secretary to the Treasury. Today it seems incredible that in 1948 it was about to be demolished. Geoffrey Houghton Brown came to the rescue, having bought it from the demolition contractor for £13,000. He then restored it with the help of one of the first Historic Buildings Council grants, acquired through the efforts of his friend Adrian Brookholding-Jones at the Ministry of Works.

Winslow Antiques, based at the Hall, bought many items from the notorious Verney 'attic' sale at nearby Claydon House, and made a killing with them. The purchase of a number of full-length family portraits led to an extraordinary incident when I arrived from London late one Friday evening to superintend the antiques business over the weekend. The key

143

turned in the door and I entered the hallway with its four symmetrically placed doors, then let out a shriek: there was a man standing in each doorway, watching me. Regaining my composure I stared again, and found that Geoffrey had cut out four full-length Highmore-style Verney portraits and tacked one onto each door, like *tromp-l'oeil*. It was a characteristic Geoffrey touch.

Winslow was well stocked, and a frequent visitor was Felix Harbord, who shared Geoffrey's taste for the exotic and decorative. In particular Felix had his eye on the rococo wood carvings by Mr Lightfoot of Claydon, for he was then decorating Chicheley Hall and Oving, both nearby county seats. Oving, only a few miles away from Winslow, had been bought by Michael and Pamela Berry from the irascible Randolph Churchill, who was most reluctant to move out. We saw his final attempted exit, in a huge pantechnicon. The driver was having great difficulty turning in the narrow forecourt, and Randolph, furious, his face glowing like hot coals (we thought he was going to explode, or have a heart attack) rushed up to the cab, violently pulled the poor man out, got in himself, and in turning crashed the pantechnicon into the eighteenth-century iron gates. He then shouted at the man cowering by the wall, uttered expletives, and disappeared indoors; we never saw him again. The man calmly got into his cab and drove away, and Pamela Berry came out to say that her chauffeur would remove Randolph.

Oving boasted a grand saloon with a rich rococo ceiling of *c.* 1740–50, to which Felix grafted on extra rococo decoration. In this he displayed genius: so convincing is it that it could easily be mistaken for the work of Thomas Roberts of Oxford, to whom the original plasterwork has been attributed. The house was now ripe for *Country Life*. Mark Girouard said he must come and make a reconnaissance; could he stay for the week-end at Winslow? Of course he could. He arrived on Saturday and telephoned the Berrys asking if we could go over on Sunday morning. 'You may come,' said Pamela Berry, 'but only for a drink. We have a large lunch party. Don't be late. Arrive at 1.00' – firm instructions that put us in our place in the social hierarchy.

We decided to walk and, looking at the map, Mark's eye was caught by Swanbourne House. I said I knew it as Victorian, and now a school, but Mark suggested we make a diversion. Swanbourne was a dour classical house in an evocative Victorian estate setting. Only when I joined the RIBA in 1956, a year later, did I discover the drawings of it by William Burn for Sir Thomas Fremantle in 1864. We went to the church, and expressed innocent surprise that morning Communion was over. Inside we gazed upon a 'Harrowing of Hell' of about 1500 with three devils or evil spirits, inscribed 'Timor Mortis'.

After Swanbourne we cut across a field, oblivious of a large brown animal grazing in the middle. Then we suddenly became aware of a huge bull, with enormous testicles pendulously swaying to and fro. From an amble, the beast changed gear and rapidly advanced. We fled helter-skelter towards the nearest hedge. Mark ran faster, and treated me to the amazing sight of a senior architectural historian, arms held high in front of his face, taking a running leap through the hedge. I behaved more decorously, squeezing through a small prickly hole, but ripped my jacket down the front.

Swanbourne and 'Old Testicle' had delayed us, but Mark mumbled that we could afford to be a little late. Passing through Oving village we saw an enticing pub, and felt we deserved a snack. It was 12.40 by our watches, so we dived in and had a sandwich and beer. Imagine our surprise when almost at once the barmaid called 'Ten minutes to closing'. We stared at each other, then turned to her for explanation. Smilingly she said, 'Bet you forgot to put the clocks forward last night!' 'Oh God, the Berrys,' Mark gasped, and we ran, almost as fast as we had from 'Old Testicle'.

Arctic draughts met us at the door of Oving House. Mark's face was scratched, I was dirty, with a torn jacket. The Berrys were furious. They had delayed their lunch, although we could not fathom why. Guests to whom we were not introduced were irritably lounging about, and we were propelled around in double-quick time by Petulant Pamela. As we left, probably no more than ten minutes later, we sighed with relief. This time we took a direct route for Winslow, and that evening, in true Marguerite Duras style, we philosophically debated the lost or gained hour. Some months later, Mark wrote his article.

22

A question of Spitfire glass

Erddig, North Wales

ERDDIG IN WALES, that romantic and prohibited house, the Untouchable among the great country houses, denied to the traveller: what was known of its condition was terrifying, and to the uninitiated it was abandoned, shuttered, and slowly sinking due to mining subsidence. But the Yorkes lived there. From 1954 onwards the refrain in my letters to Erddig was a persistent 'Let us in Simon (or Philip) Yorke', and the answer always either a 'No', or a failure even to acknowledge the letter. Of course, trespass remained a possibility, and there is a thrill in it, doing what we call a 'hit-and-run' – running away when the house looks boring, or guard dogs emerge from the stable court. But how maddening it would be to wander around Erddig and not gain access. The reward finally came by way of Alick Barratt, whose friend Martin Kenyon was a county neighbour of those eccentric and reclusive Yorkes. Suddenly an unexpected summons came from Simon Yorke for the three of us to go to Erddig. What excitement this generated!

As we approached down the lane we were confronted by neo-classical gate piers and an iron gate, slightly ajar. It might just as well have been closed, for the drive beyond was an impenetrable mass of brambles. We stared, puzzled, then looked again at the Ordnance Survey map and located another set of piers and another drive, bumpy and with deep grassy ruts. We took this, came to a wooden gate, and beyond it deeper ruts. The path betrayed no sign of regular use. We had to abandon the car and take to our feet. Our hearts leapt when the house loomed into view: long and low, its west entrance front of 1683, once pink brick, was encased in smoke-polluted ashlar. The gravel approach was thickly grassed over, and it was clear it had been many years since anyone drew up on it to ascend the curving perron of steps. The windows were dark with dirt, only the many broken panes standing out in the afternoon light. We stared at the Doric doorcase, and the uneven steps precariously dropping away at an angle. There must be another entrance. We walked about, noticing the machinery of the West Bersham Colliery that had caused the subsidence, so near. We eventually found the entrance, down a flight of fern-grown steps in a basement in the end of the range. We rang the bell.

'No sound from the chamber, no voice from the hall', we thought as we waited. Resigned, we muttered, 'Oh well, at least we can go on to Wynnstay.' But the sharp sound of a drawn bolt suddenly focused our attention. The door slowly opened, and there was the genial Simon. Not an old face, but one covered in bumps and tufts of hair around a warm smile. As Martin was about to introduce us, he was silenced by Simon's welcoming words, which seemed, by his eye contact, to be addressed to me: 'Ah! you're here for the miller's job. I'm so pleased. Come in.' We shared puzzled looks as we stared at the full-length portraits of household servants hanging in this lower hall.

Simon strode across to a large chest, opened it, and began to throw eighteenth-century waistcoats out onto the black and white paved floor. He then turned to me and said, 'Now I know who you are. If you'll agree to take the miller's job, I'll give you this Royal coat-of-arms,' and with our help he lifted out a huge stone coat-of-arms wrapped in a yellow waistcoat. 'I've got problems with the naughty boys from Wrexham. They keep smashing the windows in the mill. But I've written to the Air Ministry and asked for Spitfire glass. That'll stop them! Shall we go to the mill now?' Laughter welled up. We attempted to explain that we were here just to see the house. But the matter of the mill was suddenly forgotten, as if it had never been mentioned, and Simon led us into the main rooms of the house. We never did discover if he had suddenly recognised Martin Kenyon, or remembered why we were there. At least we were in, and he was welcoming: that was all that mattered.

The interior remains fixed in our minds. It looked as though John Meller, strolling in in 1718, or Philip Yorke in 1772, might have found books they had been reading still lying about. All seemed frozen in time, but not necessarily in decay. We could see, however, that there was something wobbly about the place: panelling was not quite in position, ceilings had slightly dropped or bulged due to seeping water from above, floors were uneven, fabrics disintegrating. As we came into the chapel vestibule two gilt side-tables with *verre églomisé* tops were singled out by Simon, who said with a chuckle, 'Look – I broke that top with a hammer when I was a boy aged four.' The hammer was still there, and so were the broken bits of glass. Our first reaction was that Simon was staging an effect. But he wasn't, as was confirmed when we entered the State Bedroom with its eighteenth-century Chinese wall-

41. Erddig, North Wales, from the overgrown garden

42. Erddig, North Wales, the carpenter's shop

paper. Through a gaping hole in the ceiling water had poured down onto the great State Bed bought in 1720; its hangings were drenched. Two boards had been placed across the top of the tester, and on them was precariously balanced a tin bath full of water. Of course it had filled and overflowed, but it had never occurred to the Yorkes to move the bed, or even to empty the bath.

We positively shook with glee and delight. Simon let us poke about the library, open cupboards, and generally wander everywhere. Then came tea in the Servants' Hall, with more portraits of servants, and decorative circles of cutlasses arranged on the ceiling. Its equipment was still of the eighteenth and nineteenth centuries. As we ate scones, we were puzzled by Simon's several enquiries as to the whereabouts of 'the boy'. All was revealed when we later passed through the saloon to the dining room. Here was the 'boy' who had missed his tea. The furniture had been pushed to one side, the carpet rolled up, and on his hands and knees washing the wooden floor was a Boy Scout, or maybe a Cub. 'He washes a room out once a week. Bob-a-Job,' chuckled Simon.

It was now made clear to us that it was time to go, and Simon bade us farewell. Our heads were reeling. Had it not been for the boy's uniform, we might have been reliving an event in Torrington's *Diary*. We poked about in stables and outhouses, discovering all the tools that maintain a garden and park, abandoned but as if preserved in aspic since the last century. As we made a circuit of the house and explored the garden, walking the length of the long canal, we had to pinch ourselves: from a distance we saw Philip Yorke, on a path from the stables, riding a penny-farthing. Even now I wonder if my memory is at fault. Was it not perhaps Philip taking a turn on his antiquated bicycle? But no – the penny-farthings are still there, under National Trust care, and the legend of Simon and Philip riding their new-fangled machines lingers on. As we left the way we had come and the gate swung shut, it was like the curtain dropping at the end of a play.

23

Damn the Pennington-Ramsdens!

Bulstrode Park, Buckinghamshire

I JOINED THE RIBA staff in 1956, and Nikolaus Pevsner encouraged me to write for the *Architectural Review*. The inspiration for the article that eventually came out in 1958, on Bulstrode Park in Buckinghamshire, came from my recollections of a foray I had made in 1946 or 1947.

It all had to do with the Long Canal in the park, a venue for fishing with Sid. We would bicycle from Uxbridge soon after dawn, taking a picnic, and spend the whole day. Carp and tench were the speciality, as usual. I was ignorant at the time of garden history, but knew the water then as belonging to the old late seventeenth-century formal gardens, rather than the Victorian house. Sid told me Humphry Repton had land-scaped the park, and near the canal was an empty thatched Reptonian *cottage orné* where we frequently sheltered from the rain (later it was pulled down by the strange international quasi-religious community who occupied the house). Sid had been given permission to fish because he was occasionally employed in the house by a sisal company in which the Ramsden family, owners of the estate, had invested heavily – I believe to their loss. When mending chairs in the library we were once shown a portfolio of architectural designs for Bulstrode through three centuries, from the time of Judge Jefferies before 1681, through the Earls and later Dukes of Portland, to the Dukes of Somerset, and finally to the Ramsden baronets of the 1880s. Now, on 16 September 1956, not as a fisherman but to examine these drawings in my professional capacity as an architectural historian, I took what John Betjeman called the Chiltern Line to Gerrards Cross, to see the house again. Sir William Pennington-Ramsden of Muncaster Castle still maintained rooms in the house and owned many of the contents.

On arrival the marvellous sweep of Repton's landscaping first had to be crossed from the Gerrards Cross-to-Beaconsfield road. An earlier architectural style was suggested by a red-brick Williamite gazebo, but quickly negated by the hot red-brick, gabled, spiky, Benjamin Ferrey house built for the 12th Duke of Somerset in 1860. A Brother of the community welcomed me.

There was the portfolio, just as I had remembered seeing it with Sid, but it now informed me that the Arts and Crafts library and other rooms in the house had been redecorated by F.C. Eden around 1900. The complete architectural story was revealed: Judge Jefferies had a Tudor great hall house, but maybe built one new range; William Bentinck, 1st Earl of Portland, was responsible for rebuilding from 1706 in a brick baroque style to designs by William Talman set in formal gardens by George London; the 2nd Earl (later 1st Duke) added the decoration of the chapel by Sebastiano Ricci after 1709; then came the 2nd Duke and the long tenure of his Duchess,

43. Bulstrode Park, Buckinghamshire,
Edwardian view from the gardens

44. Bulstrode Park, Buckinghamshire, the Wyatt tower

that Margaret Harley who was celebrated here as Prior's 'Noble, lovely little Peggy', and created a shell museum, a menagerie, a 'Turkish pavilion', and a grotto designed by her friend Mrs Delany. There followed the incomplete rebuilding from 1802 for the 3rd Duke by James Wyatt, resulting in a strange bastard half Talman, half Wyatt castellated house; its sale in 1810 to the 11th Duke of Somerset, for whom a bevy of architects unsuccessfully competed to complete it; and after this Duke's death in 1855, the building of the new house by Ferrey for the 12th Duke in 1860. Finally, when the 12th Duke died in 1885, Bulstrode passed to his youngest daughter, Lady Helen St Maur, who had married Sir John William Ramsden in 1865.

I traced out the formal London gardens, following their turf outlines and embankments with the aid of two engraved Portland views. On the axis of the avenues that extended towards the transverse long canal was a brick tower with octagonal turrets at the angles, and a mullioned-windowed room above. It was Wyatt's towered entrance to the main courtyard of his castellated house, but after the Somersets demolished this it stood isolated, looking like a water-tower on four open arches. Ascent was all too inviting, so I hastily forced my way in and climbed the spiral stairs to the first-floor room. My eyes boggled at what I saw: a still-life of objects that had seemingly been in place for years. The floor was covered in straw. A pair of nineteenth-century rococo mirrors, the gilt falling off the white gesso, was propped against a wall. In front of a second wall were three portraits of a Hudson or Highmore sort, their canvases all torn, maybe left-overs from the last Portland duke; and in a tin box were the mathematical papers of the 11th Duke of Somerset, who had written a *Treatise on the Relative Elementary Properties of the Ellipse and the Circle*. Round about were piles of mildewed books, all eighteenth-century, several with the book plate of the Dukes of Somerset. It was like past centuries seen through a looking glass, the sisal occupants, the Brotherhood, even Sir William Ramsden, apparently oblivious of the survival of this distillation of history so near them.

The Ramsdens subsequently fell upon hard times, as did so many families who possessed several seats. They had Turweston in Oxfordshire, Ardverikie in Scotland, and Byram Hall in Yorkshire, with its great neo-classical library, which was demolished in 1922. They had also inherited Muncaster Castle, Cumberland, in 1917. They were forced to sell the best of the contents of Bulstrode in 1932, and in July 1958 occurred the second sale, of the 'Remaining Contents of the Mansion' – but I was surprised to find, when I attended the sale, that the portfolio of drawings I had consulted in 1956 was not included. This was followed that November by my article, and I sent a copy of it to the Brotherhood, as a courtesy. Imagine my surprise when I later received a letter from Sir William Pennington-Ramsden of Muncaster Castle, asking whether I still had the portfolio of drawings. He did not exactly accuse me of taking them, but I read as much into his unfortunately-worded letter. 'Damn the Pennington-Ramsdens!' I thought to myself. I assumed he had learned of my article from the Brotherhood, and had wondered, as I had, why the drawings had not been in the sale. The years passed, and I often ruminated on the whereabouts of that portfolio. If the drawings had been stolen, they would eventually appear at auction or with a book dealer.

I visited Bulstrode again in the late 1970s, attracted by a fête in the park. The house was open to the public, and without bothering to identify myself I asked a Brother in charge if he had ever seen the drawings. 'Oh!' he said, 'we believe they were taken by someone who wrote about the house.' I was stuttering with an ire which still coloured a visit I made to Bulstrode twenty years later, with Tim, Todd and Eileen. We found the house abandoned by the Brotherhood and now run by Evangelical Christians, all friendly 'Hi there', Christ-children taught by good, sandalled teachers with brown toes in hideously-painted classrooms, Evangelical arts and crafts. The matter of the drawings still rankled, and my fury can be imagined when less than a month later Christie's asked for my opinion on some 'Wyatville and Sandys' drawings *from this portfolio*, reputedly consigned by 'someone in New York'. I subsequently learned from a friend that the drawings had always been in the possession of the Pennington-Ramsdens, and had been touted about by an agent to ascertain their value. 'Damn them,' I thought again. The same portfolio, sent from Muncaster Castle but lacking many of the drawings I saw in 1956, was sold at Sotheby's in April 1997.

24

Into the arms of the tart next door

Bure Homage and Highcliffe Castle, Hampshire

I LL–FATED BURE Homage was built for the Baronne de Feuchères about 1835 by W.J. Donthorn, who five years earlier had designed Gothic Highcliffe Castle for Lord Stuart de Rothesay. Both were Hampshire seats enjoying a marine prospect, but more pertinently, their estates were contiguous. They also came to share the same predicament, strangled by encroaching development. So forgotten is Bure Homage (it was demolished in 1957) that when David Lloyd wrote *Hampshire* for Pevsner in 1966 he seemed oblivious of the fact that it had ever existed, only describing a neighbouring house called Sandhills as 'Derelict' at the time of writing, 'facing caravans rather than the sea'. His comment encapsulates the disdain that Christchurch Borough Council displayed in those days towards historic buildings under their care. For me, Bure has more modern associations: in a telephone box in Paddington Street, W1, with advertisements for alluring ladies, one offered 'Gas masks a speciality'. Its relevance will become apparent.

On the way to Highcliffe Castle in the summer of 1955 I took a train to see Christchurch Priory, to wonder not only at the Countess of Salisbury's chantry and the chancel reredos, but also at that affecting monument to Shelley, lying sculpted (in 1854) in Weekes's white marble with his head in the lap of a girl, a monument originally intended for St Peter's, Bournemouth, where his heart is buried. I then made my way to Purwell and Mudeford, a short beach-stroll from Highcliffe.

Just how entwined Bure and Highcliffe were, I had no idea. I did not know that the 3rd Earl of Bute's classical Georgian Highcliffe was demolished in 1794 by his fourth son, Lord Charles Stuart, who retained a farmhouse, Bure Homage, renamed by him Bure Cottage. This he left to *his* son, also Charles, who was our ambassador in Paris for two terms (1815–1824 and, as Lord Stuart de Rothesay, 1828–1831). His mother-in-law, the Countess of Hardwick, had described Bure as 'a sweet little bird's nest', little knowing, one supposes, how relevant this description would prove. For Lord Stuart de Rothesay was not only a great collector but also a great philanderer, and it would appear that it was he who sold the 'bird's nest' to the delectably ravishing tart Sophia Daw, who as the Baronne de Feuchères, the Duc de Bourbon's notoriously lascivious mistress, had been known as 'the Queen of Chantilly'. Long since abandoned by her legitimate husband, she rebuilt Bure Homage out of the two million francs bequeathed to her by Bourbon. Can one really believe she was not Lord Stuart de Rothesay's mistress as well? How convenient for him to walk across from Highcliffe to Bure, and into her arms.

However, on that summer's day in 1955 all this was unknown to me. I would have passed Bure by had I not glimpsed its pilastered elevation at the end of a street of dull houses in this seaside village of Mudeford. My architectural proboscis, even in its then undeveloped state, quivered. I emerged from a built-up suburbia of undistinguished boarding-houses and bed-sits to be confronted by Bure, a decaying monument of the Greek Revival encircled by development since 1939. Donthorn had carefully studied the works of the great German architect Schinkel, and Schinkel himself could not have done better. There, in a minimal garden, was the astonishing Bure, wrapped around by a high security fence. It had been owned by the Ricardo family since the late nineteenth century; Frank Ricardo sold the contents in 1938, the house was auctioned for development the following year, then plans were abandoned because of the onset of war. I was determined to breach its defences.

First I discreetly negotiated the perimeter, feeling somewhat conspicuous. The gate was padlocked, with the wire brought right close to the ground, except – and this was the Achilles' heel of the security services – in one far corner which caught my eye, where some local lad had bent up the wire and it had then been turned down again. So I eyed the road, lifted the wire surreptitiously, prostrated myself at full length, and wiggled through in triumph on my tummy.

Only now can I appreciate Donthorn's masterful enwrapping of the house with the Greek orders of architecture, inspired by 'Athenian' Stuart and Nicholas Revett's *Antiquities of Athens* or Revett's *Antiquities of Ionia*. It was not as powerful as The Grange, which Donthorn knew, but it was as good.

As a house it was really no more than a bungalow writ large, just a sequence of spacious but few ground floor rooms. I had to hide furtively in the portico, then scamper unseen (I hoped) along each façade, until I found a shuttered window that opened – and I was in. (Gervase Jackson-Stops once laughingly said that if I were ever ennobled, my motto should

45. Bure Homage, Hampshire, north front, 1955

46. Highcliffe Castle, Hampshire, north entrance

be 'Up, over and in'.) In truth, I remember little detail: fire
notices here and there concerning the Royal Corps of Signals
and the US Air Force, fire extinguishers, bare floorboards –
but there was one marvellous floor in mahogany with inlaid
flower patterns, such as I later noticed in some early nineteenth-century Austro-Hungarian houses. There was a
Greekly domed hall and a stair winding up to Greek bas-reliefs
running round the walls, and a pretty circular glazed dome
to the hall; upstairs were the ubiquitous iron beds. In the
dining room a huge fitted Regency serving table had survived
vandals. I remember only its large claw feet. Nothing unusual
so far – until I entered the library: on the floor, a scatter of US
Air Force papers, presumably bumph pertinent to D-Day; but
on the shelves, a surreal composition that today would be per-
petuated with my Leica. In one bay, arranged on five shelves
were twenty gas masks, each under a US tin helmet, four to a
shelf. Full marks to the joker of Bure, I thought. Later, when I
knew more, I reflected that had she lived into the twentieth
century, Sophia Daw might also have advertised 'Gas masks a
speciality'.

Under the wire again and out, past bed-and-breakfasts to the
groynes and the sea walk to Highcliffe, a mile or so away. In a
sense, I wish I had never gone there. Apart from the drama of
the entrance porch and the Great Hall, reminiscent of William
Beckford's Fonthill or the Duke of Bridgewater's Ashridge,
Highcliffe has always seemed an unsatisfactory composition, as
if Lord Stuart de Rothesay himself had taken a hand in the
design, as I suspect he did. Of course, I later came to appreciate the archaeological interest of identifying the medieval bits
and pieces he brought back from France. Only two years
before my visit the Castle had been sold by the family to the

Claretian Fathers, who in my eyes, if not in the eyes of God, were vandals. They ripped out the spectacular staircase in the Great Hall, so setting in train a pattern of destruction only recently halted by state grants with the reluctant co-operation of Christchurch Borough Council. It was all very different in 1876, when Augustus Hare wrote: 'I have left Highcliffe, and the gates of Paradise seem closed.'

25

Cells for Nazis and Pugin papers

Willingham House and Bayons Manor, Lincolnshire

I'M SURPRISED THAT I never youth-hostelled through Lin-colnshire – but the motorists who stopped for me never seemed to be going in that direction. I always seemed to be on the wrong side of the river Trent. Yet I had visited the county before I chose it for the *Buildings of England* series and became enamoured of it. In making that choice I had one house in mind – Bayons Manor – and the catalyst was an upholstery job Sid had at a house opposite Market Rasen race course, for an owner who had been a solicitor in Uxbridge. We were put up in Market Rasen, arriving there from London via Lincoln and a change to a long-axed rural line connecting with Grimsby by way of halts with names such as Snelland and Wickenby, Usselby and Moortown.

I was in the fortnight's hiatus between leaving Collin and Winslow and joining the RIBA Library, so it must have been April 1956. It was a cold spring – that I remember. Sid worked, I walked: to a tumulus in the woods at Chapel

47. Willingham House,
Lincolnshire, south front,
1959

48. Willingham House,
Lincolnshire, west front,
1959

49. Willingham House, Lincolnshire, staircase, November 1961

Hill, and to Dog Kennel Farm, where I found early nineteenth-century kennels. Two discoveries puzzled me: a trench-like enclosure with a fitting that might have suited a bren-gun, and an old Ministry of Defence notice, its flaking paint warning the reader not to pass by. This was my first encounter with Willingham House, even then nearly engulfed by close forestry planting. A large notice proclaimed the Lindsey Division of the Civil Defence. It was a training centre, in the shadow of the Cold War (the City of Bath issued handbells to announce an imminent nuclear attack). The place seemed abandoned, and no one accosted me.

The impressions conveyed in the piece I eventually wrote about Willingham in 1959 (published in 1964) were more knowledgeably ordered than those I received at the time. The house was built for an Ayscough Boucherett in 1790. 'Its neo-classical quality proclaims a London architect,' I wrote, attributing it to Robert Mitchell: its four-column Ionic portico with Coade stone capitals had a very metropolitan look, as did the pilaster portico on the side front. Inside, a beautiful iron stair wound up around a tall, light space, ornamented with neo-classical friezes. My memory of the plasterwork decoration of the ceiling remains clear: it was a masterpiece of the sharpest and finest ornament, and could only have been executed by a top plasterer. At the bottom of the stairs an anachronistic note was struck by racks with dozens of tin helmets, and a pile of fire blankets and coils of rope on the floor. I went upstairs, still unchallenged, then up further into the attics, where I made an unusual discovery: two rooms had windows with thick iron bars and strengthened doors. Had this been a lunatic asylum? Then I saw names and dates written in German on the wall. I returned downstairs to look in the larger rooms – all with their elegant decoration, and sophisticated

50. Bayons Manor, Lincolnshire, garden front, 1959

51. Bayons Manor, Lincolnshire,
portcullis entrance with JH, 1959

52. Bayons Manor, Lincolnshire, chimney-piece, 1959

53. Bayons Manor, Lincolnshire, chimney-piece, 1959

chimney-pieces by a London sculptor. Still no one barred me. It was uncanny but, as I was beginning to find, commonplace. I walked back to Sid, to be told that during the war Willingham had housed first German prisoners-of-war, then Italian. No doubt the attic cells were for recalcitrant Nazis.

'If you like ruins,' said Sid's employer, 'go to Bayons Manor a couple of miles up the road.' I did, and this pseudo-medieval castle with gatehouses and battlements, baileys and barbicans, left an impression on me unlike any other I had experienced. The place was deserted, used only as a trysting place for local snoggers. When the Duke of Northumberland visited Bayons about 1845, he remarked to Charles Tennyson (who in the best baronial taste had added 'd'Eyncourt' to his name), 'At Alnwick I have only three gateways, *you* have six.' Tennyson conceived the picturesque whole himself, with the help of professionals, notably Anthony Salvin and W.A. Nicholson, between 1836 and 1840: the result must have astounded his retainers. In 1956 trees were growing out of curtain walls, the adjacent ancillary buildings had collapsed in a jumble of timbers, and the whole looked ready to return to Nature. It was truly the enchanted palace of the Sleeping Beauty, 'a fairy-tale invention' wrote Mark Girouard. I wandered through room after room, Pugin papers fluttering off the walls, the hammer-beamed Great Hall a wreck, panelling ripped off and splintered, wonderful carved stone Puginesque chimney-pieces defaced. Geoffrey Houghton Brown's antique dealer from Grantham had carted off a load of Gothic furniture some years before. Upstairs, birds fluttered and cawed at my presence. I thought then, and later wrote: 'Bayons is now in total decay, and never looked better.' In 1959 the situation had changed little since my first visit, the decay simply more picturesque,

Nature taking the upper hand. The house had become one with its choking greenery, the birds more numerous. The only difference was that a local group of motor-cyclists, leather-clad ton-up boys, had discovered the joys of roaring around the gardens, through the portcullises, even in and out of the rooms. In the revised edition of *Lincolnshire* by Nicholas Antram in 1989, the comment is made, 'tragically demolished in 1965. Its replacement needs no comment.' It was a bungalow: I would have written something much stronger.

26

Laments and curses

Watnall Hall and Bulwell Hall, Nottinghamshire

I FOUND IN the RIBA a drawing of Nuthall Temple in the environs of Nottingham. In cataloguing it I learned of the tragic demolition in 1929 of a house that merited comparison with Palladian Chiswick or Mereworth. Its soaring plasterwork domed hall, one of the glories of English rococo decoration, was comparable to the fantasy of Bavarian rococo. Did anything remain? I wondered. With the drawing tucked in my bag I set off in 1957 for Nottingham, and by bus through suburbs blighted by coal mining to Nuthall, a remnant of a village now sliced through by the cacophonous M1. It was impossible to believe that a great Palladian villa could have stood here: the reduced area of park was strangled, the lake polluted, and the Gothic summer-house by Thomas Wright, Nuthall's architect (1759), decaying. At that time Thomas Wright, architect, garden designer and 'Wizard astronomer of Durham', was unknown to any of us, even Howard Colvin.

My trip was in vain, as I had feared. Should I return to

the city centre and visit the Castle Museum? I had with me Pevsner's *Nottinghamshire* (1951), and noticed the nearby village of Watnall Chaworth. 'Watnall': that struck a chord. Pevsner wrote of a 'fine brick building of *c.* 1690 or 1700', mentioning also iron gates by Huntingdon Shaw (in fact, he was perpetuating a myth), the best in the county. There were no gates, but on the terrace were old RAF huts; the garden was a rubbish tip; the house was empty, the bulldozers waiting to pounce. How could they? Here was as perfect a Williamite composition as one could hope for, apart from a later porch and wing. The Rolleston family sold up in 1954, and the Nottingham developers had moved in fast. Once the house had been abandoned, windows had been smashed, the door forced open. As I walked in, the full tragedy of the situation hit me. The interior was perfection: suites of distinguished panelled rooms, simple bolection chimney-pieces, reserved plasterwork, and quite the finest staircase of its date anywhere in the county. I climbed out onto the roof to stand amazed at the far-reaching views, once pastoral, now all in a smoky haze, corrupted by coal mining, and smoke-belching factories. As I left, in drove a bulldozer. Lamenting, I caught a bus to the city.

No sooner had the bus moved off and on its way through mining slums and scarred colliery fields than in Pevsner his mention of Bulwell Hall took my eye. I quickly consulted the map, and in ten minutes I was off the bus and following the track of a mining railway, then over a bridge across the main Nottingham-to-Derby line, to weave my way across unappetising derelict land to a house long since abandoned for domestic use. Pevsner gave it four lines, and from what he wrote he can hardly have seen it first-hand: it was then an Approved School. From the ugly stable range a questioning

54. Watnall Hall, Nottinghamshire, from the terraced garden

55. Watnall Hall, Nottinghamshire, the library, 1955

56. Bulwell Hall, Nottinghamshire, east entrance front, 1958

57. Bulwell Hall, Nottinghamshire, entrance hall, 1958

woman emerged, then disappeared to fetch her caretaker husband. 'Go in at yer own risk,' he said, in a dialect that might just as well have been a foreign language. 'It's coming down in any case.' And he gave me a key to the front door.

First I stood looking up at the entrance elevation. The house had been built by John Newton in 1770 in old-fashioned Palladian taste. All the large extensions to right and left were by a Victorian owner, Samuel Cooper, as was the coarse ornamentalising of the Georgian façade. Every pane of glass had been smashed, and when I entered the hall I was confronted by rooms ransacked from top to bottom. The chimney-pieces were all gone, except for one, deliberately smashed up as if with a sledge-hammer, the stair balustrade had been ripped out, and panels of brightly-coloured Crace-style (maybe Edwardian) decoration in the dining room had been scored through, apparently with some sort of blade. 'God,' I thought, 'what a horrible place.' On the walls in the attic were scribbled Italian names and place-names, a poignant record of the Italian prisoners-of-war who had been held here. It was hard to believe the grounds had ever been 'ornamental', or boasted a seven-acre lake, or indeed that this dismal house had contained Mr Cooper's respectable collection of French, Dutch and Italian pictures. Yet on the periphery of the park I found a strangely comical lodge with a semi-circular gable. As I passed the stables and thanked the caretaker, I sensed nasty vibes. It was time to go: and as I did so, I cursed the place, so horrible was it. I returned to Nottingham, to examine the architectural model of the Castle in the museum.

27

Of sheep and potatoes

Burwell Park, Lincolnshire

THERE CAN BE nothing better than old editions of the one-inch Ordnance Survey maps to show the disposition of the parks of Britain; the new (1991) Landranger editions are such a sad travesty. On the earlier maps, each park was coloured grey, to its original boundaries. Travelling through Lincolnshire in 1957, I found the flat fenland cartographically devoid of grey; and then, where the hilly Wolds begin, almost as an elevated land barrier to the Holland of the south, grey parks begin to proliferate. Radiating from this 'edge' above Spilsby may be found the parks of Gunby, Scremby, Langton, Aswardby and Grebby; and further towards Louth, the modest mansions of Oxcombe, Worlaby, Walmsgate, South Ormsby.

The Wolds around Oxcombe and Farforth have remained as they were when Lord Tennyson was a child, a remote place of narrow lanes and secluded combes. In 1957 I puttered my Lambretta to the top of a ridge and was rewarded by a glimpse of a red brick house. (Such sudden glimpses can tug at the

58. Burwell Park, Lincolnshire, entrance front

59. Burwell Park, Lincolnshire, staircase

60. Burwell Park, Lincolnshire, drawing-room, 1957

61. Burwell Park, Lincolnshire,
south-east room

heart; sometimes the garden surrounding a house is proclaimed by the tall outline of coniferous planting.) I had spied Burwell Park, standing monumentally atop high ground by Burwell Wood. At a time when landowners despaired of maintaining their family seats as a viable asset, the scene that met me at Burwell was the familiar one of broken windows, dereliction, and decayed gardens with a scattering of refuse. Lincolnshire anyway was a county of philistine farmers, as it still is: no place for Georgian aesthetes or fogies bleating about preservation, as was obvious once I opened the door.

But first I must marry my recollection of what I saw to my retrospective evaluation. I was confronted by one of the most perfect houses of its date in England. Built of immaculately crafted brick, it was seven bays by five with a pedimented three-bay frontispiece, the proportions of void to wall perfect, and the glazing bars original. But – as Pevsner was fond of saying when he had nothing written on his clipboard – 'Its architectural history remains to be elucidated'. The only fact to conjure with was that it had been built about 1760 by Matthew Lister. His ancestor Sir Matthew Lister, the Royal Physician, bought the estate in 1641 and was buried here in 1656. And the Listers remained here for two more centuries. In 1883 they sold out to the Grantham ironworker William Hornsby, who amazingly left the house alone. In 1949 the estate was farmed by Mr R.E. Boothby. Then it was taken over by Muckton Estates Ltd, to whom the philistine Lindsey County Council willingly gave Listed Building consent for demolition.

It was now there occurred one of the oddest things I have ever experienced at any country house. Outside the place was deserted, but as I stood on the threshold I could hear shuffling inside. So it was occupied. I knocked, and heard more shuffling, then knocked again and called out; but the response was the same shuffling. I tried the door, it opened – and suddenly, as if caught up in a torrent, I was engulfed by a flock of sheep. They shot across the brambled lawn and disappeared into a field. Conditions inside beggared belief, for the floor of the hall was awash with stinking muck and urine. How on earth did they get in there? Had one got in and the others followed, and the door blown shut? Or had they been put in there as a temporary measure? If so, I had let them out ... I looked furtively around, but no Muckton farmer appeared to upbraid me.

But the decoration! The Doric entablature was bold, and the ceilings were of Gibbsian derivation. I stared incredulously at the Palladian overmantel frame, still with its eighteenth-century 'view'. In the staircase hall, with its floor of white marble with inset black squares, I gasped at the perfect ensemble. Two hundred years of occupation had added nothing except antlers and stag's heads, presumably Hornsby's, on the walls. The stair was of superlative mahogany construction, serpentining up at the angles, with elegant balusters. Plaster perfection continued in the drawing room, the dining room, and every other room, and the attic rooms were as the builder had left them in 1760. In several rooms were hundreds of sacks of potatoes and mountainous heaps of grain (no more sheep), and family portraits were hanging on the walls, covered in cobwebs, an added theatricality.

Years later, when I understood how rare a survival these rooms were, I recognised their style as Palladian laced with rococo decoration, the patterns similar to those in Abraham Swan's *The British Architect* (1745) or his *Collection of Designs in Architecture* (1757). Indeed, Burwell's interior was a perfect demonstration of the use of these books. Yet it was not merely copyist, but stood apart from the average provincial county work; indeed, it was not so very inferior to the work of Sir Robert Taylor. The wall frames and window heads in one room were in the form of a scrolled pediment clasping a shell, a motif found in a more sophisticated context in a room in Lincoln of exactly the same date, attributed to Sir William Chambers.

I left bemused by it all, and despite many enquiries failed to find out anything more about Burwell. Then in April 1958 my county friend Froude Dillon Trollope-Bellew, of Casewick Hall near Stamford, pressed me to return hurriedly. He had heard that Burwell was to be demolished — 'if it hasn't gone already'. I came the same way, topped the same ridge — but this time something was wrong. Where had the roof beyond the trees gone to? The drive was deeply rutted, and there was an acrid smell of burning. What a sight met my eyes! The roof was off, and about a third of the house was gone, leaving a series of rooms, like steps from top to bottom, exposed to the open air as hollow or broken cubes. I remembered London in the Blitz. Silhouetted on the skyline were three men with picks precariously hacking away at the rococo plasterwork and bricks. I just stood there watching plaster decoration fall to the ground. They gave me six heads, which I stuffed in my pannier: Felix Harbord bought them from me. On the lawn lay a pile of chimney-piece overmantels, panelling, and the black-and-white marble floor, which had been prised up. On a side terrace a crackling bonfire consumed the sawn-up stairs and timber beams. I was black with rage. As a single act of destruction, the burning of a masterpiece from the National Gallery would have been no worse.

28

But where are the golfers?

Dyrham Park, Hertfordshire and Wrotham Park, Middlesex

M Y FAVOURITE ONE-INCH Ordnance Survey maps are the four that cover the environs of London. On the northern pair, I was always intrigued by the rurality of an area bounded by Barnet to the south, Potters Bar to the north, Boreham Wood to the west and Enfield to the east. The eastern third was covered by Enfield Chase, but between Potters Bar and Boreham Wood two parks stood out as contiguous: Dyrham Park and Wrotham Park. Even today this rurality has survived, although the A1 skirting Dyrham has now been upgraded and the accursed M25 forms the northern boundary of both parks.

I turned to William Keane's *The Beauties of Middlesex: Being a Particular Description of the Principal Seats of the Nobility and Gentry*, printed in Chelsea in 1850, to compare his account with Pevsner's *Middlesex* (1951). Pevsner had obviously not consulted Keane, for his facts were wrong: Captain Trotter's Dyrham had burnt down in 1806, and had been rebuilt.

Keane's comment about how the landscape of Dyrham connects to the 'rich scenery' of Wrotham persuaded me to seek out these two houses on a ramble starting at High Barnet station. I was also encouraged by a comment in *The Ambulator* (1806) upon the 'magnificent gateway' built by Christopher Bethel, Trotter's predecessor, 'at a cost of £2,000'.

I remember walking through Barnet, finding Gallery Lane and stopping at an old moated site, Fold Farm, then discovering the western entrance to Dyrham. The way was barred, but this was no monumental gate: up and over was no problem. An aura of decay bespoke the forsaken house that loomed near. As I moved forward I found I was at the back of the house, which might have been pre-fire. Around the corner on the north front was the noble Vitruvian Tuscan portico that Pevsner rightly compares to St Paul's, Covent Garden – obviously by Captain Trotter's unknown architect, in 1806. The east front was pedimented and the south front had an ample bow – all with Tuscan eaves. An open door on one side gave me hope, but it led into a battered room with Pompeian frieze decoration, the inner door of which was well and truly boarded up. So I retreated to the back of the house again. Here a sash window yielded to my attentions, and I was in. A passage and a door opened into a remarkable pilastered Greek Ionic two-storey hall, one wall of the upper range open as a corridor. What took my eye here, apart from a mountain of paper refuse, was the splendid Palladian white veined marble chimney-piece with terms. Unless it had been imported from elsewhere, it must have come from the earlier house belonging to the Bethel family. Alas, all the communicating doors out of this hall were locked: annoyingly, I could go no further.

Keane was enamoured of the park, and his description tallied with what I saw in every particular, except that he had

62. Dyrham Park, Hertfordshire, portico with hunt

63. Dyrham Park, Hertfordshire, entrance gates, 1955

entered by the monumental Tuscan gateway at the north-east boundary. I reversed his route. The lake bounded by a grove of pines, the bridge, and the sweep of the designed landscape were all in place, and I could join him in his view across the valley to the wooded heights of Wrotham Park. As I left the grand gate with its flanking pavilions I agreed with Pevsner that it belonged to the later eighteenth century and was, as *The Ambulator* indicated, Mr Bethel's £2,000-commission. I later learned, in the course of a frustrated search for photographs of Dyrham in its desuetude, that it had become a golf club.

Wrotham, I had been told, was already a golf club. Leaving Dyrham and crossing the A1081 at Dancers Hill Road, I could enter the park on the corner of Kitts End Road. A plain wooden gate was not very auspicious; obviously it was not the main entrance. The golf course must be beyond the woods I was walking through; I remember the path turning to the right, and a sheet of water on the left. Suddenly I was on the edge of a formal garden in the Edwardian architectural style. Was this formerly the site of Keane's 'pleasure grounds and flower gardens', I wondered. In the centre of one box-enclosed area was the stone Byng Mausoleum. From here the north end of the house loomed up. Opening my Pevsner, it became obvious that he had never visited the place, which surprised me, as golf clubs are usually accessible. I walked round past terrace works to the west or garden front with its grand Ionic portico and domed pavilions, and could distinguish the effects of the restitution work, after a fire in 1883, to the 'villa' built by Isaac Ware in 1754 for Admiral Byng. The park extended to the horizon. What immaculate gardens for a golf club – but where were the golfers?

I had now gone all around the house and was under the Ionic portico of the north or entrance front: I would go in, and find the Secretary. In the centre of a grandly Ionic hall was a large circular table standing on an entwined dolphin support, suggesting an allusion to the Admiral. But my brows wrinkled: here was much fine furniture, good pictures, valuable objects, all bespeaking an unusually lavishly-maintained club house. The dark marbleised classical 1880s decor certainly conveyed a club-like ambience. Now, where was the Secretary's office? I walked through a vestibule, past grand stairs, and into a long dining room hung with Edwardian portraits, silver on the table, fruit on the sideboard. Then the horror of the situation dawned, the absence of golfers was explained – David Vicary had misinformed me, and the well-maintained gardens, the domestic and private appurtances, the elegant table silver, all proclaimed the private house of old Mrs Byng. Drained with fright I hesitated, then hastily beat a retreat, left the portico and walked down the main drive expecting at any moment to hear a voice commanding me to stop. No voice hailed me. I had come and I had gone, and sleepy old Mrs Byng was none the wiser. Wrotham remains today the largest house in private occupation in the environs of London.

29

An arcadia in the rural Wolds

Sturton Hall and Panton Hall, Lincolnshire

THERE ARE AS many deserted airfields as lost houses ringing Lincoln – and there is often a cause-and-effect link between the presence of the RAF or USAF during the Second World War and a house in crisis. Branston Hall and Longhills were subservient to Metheringham airfield, Hartsholme to Hartsholme, Tupholme to Bardney, Fillingham to Ingham, Hackthorne to Scampton. If war use never led to actual demolition, it tended to exacerbate disuse and decay.

From Lincoln I was making for Panton Hall. I stopped briefly at Snarford to absorb the atmosphere of the site of the long-lost Jacobean mansion of Sir George St Paul, then glimpsed a barn at Goltho, all that marks the site of the Granthams' tall brick Williamite house with its tall stone piers supporting great urns, demolished as long ago as 1812. From Wragby I diverted a mile or two onto the Horncastle Road to Great Sturton, intrigued by what I had read of Sturton Hall and Joseph Montague Livesey, who had enlarged his plain

64. Sturton Hall, Lincolnshire, the stables, 1959

65. Sturton Hall, Lincolnshire,
ruins of the garden front, 1959

late-Georgian family seat of 1810 in a vigorous Italianate style in 1873. His conservatories and vineries were famous, and I hoped to find out more about his much-vaunted collection of stuffed birds and animals, one his favourite lion Nero, no less, perhaps a mate of the pet lion at Haverholme Priory. Alas, I was too late: all that was left was a gutted ruin and a handsome brick stable block and farm buildings in the style of William Legg.

I have never loved anywhere more than the narrow lanes and remote hamlets of the high Wolds. From Great Sturton I drove to Sotby (its church disused) and came over Warren Hill to the hamlet of Panton. Its tiny church of St Andrew was also disused and, like the one at Dogmersfield in Hampshire, had nearly disappeared in encroaching ivy, its interior in chaos. Passing a moated cottage, I came to Goddard Hill, noted the estate buildings, then instead of entering Panton Hall by the main drive through Lodge Covert, preferred a rear assault, giving me a view across the miniature park. I was struck by a sense of planted design, later confirmed when I found a reference to William Eames as Carr's landscape gardener. What struck me even more as I made my way through the parkland was the splendid positioning of the tall brick house atop a high ridge, with distant views across the wide Wolds from both the main fronts. The ambience was magical.

In his 1954 *Dictionary* Howard Colvin credited Panton Hall to John Carr, built for Edward Turnor in 1775, despite Angus's comment in his *Seats* in 1787 that Carr was at that time making additions to a house designed for Joseph Gace *c.* 1720 by Nicholas Hawksmoor. This was tantalising, and I was yearning to inspect Panton, particularly as I now had some new information that complicated the issue: the eminent scholar Margaret Whinney had been told by a member of the

66. Panton, Lincolnshire, St Andrew's church, December 1972

67. Panton Hall, Lincolnshire, from the park, 1957

Turnor family that designs by William Talman for Panton once existed.

As I walked up to the house, noting its dominant relationship to the even grander stables at a slightly lower level, trouble began. From those grand brick stables two large collies made a barking bee-line for me, accompanied by an equally ferocious elderly labourer, shouting something about 'Keep Out' signs on the lodge gate. Once the general ferocity had diminished, however, the man proved well-informed about the house, becoming positively friendly. He was the caretaker, when he was not attending to his pigs. As I explained my interest in the architectural history, he cottoned on immediately, knew the wings had been added, and told me that blocked-up windows had been found on the inner walls of the main house. He said the Turnors had sold up in 1917 to Sir John Marsden, who left the house empty, preferring to live in a flat in the stables. The Turnors now lived at Little Ponton Hall – 'But', he added provocatively (at least that was my tingling feeling), 'ha, ha! don't let the daughter get at you. She's a right one!'

I had read Maurice Barley's sympathetic *Lincolnshire and the Fens*, written in 1952 when Panton was 'falling into decay'. Today we are so adept at finding new uses for large houses that Panton would surely have found willing occupants. Having housed a Franciscan school during the war, it stood empty after 1945. Farming had continued around it during the war years and the stables (1777, by the same Legg responsible for Sturton) were in constant use. The caretaker, now an ally, gave me a key to the house. Some years earlier the back forecourt had been netted off and the ground floor rooms used as chicken coops: some were black with dried droppings. There was a handsome white marble Carr chimney-piece in the hall, and fine but plain chimney-pieces in most of the rooms. These were not elaborately decorated, but that was the attraction: all were wondrously reserved. The house had not been tampered with since Carr's day. The bedrooms upstairs could only be described as windows on the Arcadia of the rural Wolds. The only room up here showing signs of occupation was piled high with iron bedsteads.

Carr had obviously done a complete interior redecoration, but as I stood in the hall and noticed how the dark, low-ceilinged space opened up into the high-lit staircase with a screen of columns, I realised that this was a spatial device favoured by Talman, as was the oval room leading to the garden, one end pushing into the canted bay just like the centre of his design for Castle Howard. I came here again to see the house when it was half-demolished, and it confirmed everything: the tall central block with its powerful canted bay rising three storeys *was* the original Gace house, and the wings with their canted bays to the ends, answering the centre, *were* by Carr. When I went to look through the Turnor papers I did not find the Talman drawings; nor, alas, did I see the daughter – who perhaps had been locked away because of my presence. The original house was obviously by Talman, and at his death in November 1719 Gace clearly brought in Hawksmoor for the finishings. It all made sense.

I came here once more, in April 1997, with my son Luke. The 'Keep Out' notices were still there, but we walked through the old Eames park to the rising site of the house, its cellars now filled in. The prospect of the Wolds was as captivating as in 1959, and as we looked down to the grand stables, shuttered and boarded up, we thought what a fine house they would make.

30

Of condoms and a grand piano

Uffington House, Lincolnshire

IT WAS 1958, and to escape from the boredom of abstracting references in the library of the Society of Antiquaries for Pevsner's *Lincolnshire*, I decided to make a Lambretta reconnaissance, seeking out ruined houses and lost gardens. I had already made note of half a dozen promising sites I was determined to explore, even if Pevsner thought I was wasting my time.

I set off from the sybaritic comfort of the George Inn at Stamford, then as now one of the most luxurious hostelries in England. (Not to Pevsner's taste: he preferred spartan boarding-houses, and even wrote an article about minimal needs for travellers.) Leaving Stamford, that perfect Georgian pattern-book town, I took the Deeping Road to call on old Froude Dillon Trollope-Bellew at Casewick Hall, one of the unknown houses of England, itself deserving notice for its charming Strawberry Hill Gothick front. Froude had promised me information about the location of a Tudor garden he had found in the eastern fens.

As so often happened, the unexpected brought me up sharp – at Uffington, where stone gate-piers to the church were mirrored across the road by grander ones with iron gates, theatrically screening an overgrown yew avenue through which could be glimpsed a provocative perspective of statues. The adrenalin flowed! My notes say simply, 'Charles Bertie 1681–86. Fire 1904. C. Life xvi, 992. Lady Muriel Barclay Harvey'. I recognised the gates as of about 1700 and quite the best in the county, probably by John Lumley of nearby Burley-on-the-Hill, Rutland as they were identical to ones at that great house.

I discovered that the main 'Georgian' (in fact Edwardian) lodges to the east were shut, so a furtive flanking attack was necessary, scaling a farm gate, slinking past a cottage window and a range of ruined stables in the Early Georgian Baroque style of George Portwood's Stamford. Turning the corner, I was confronted by a Baroque Revival garden entrance opening to a grassed terrace, the sad site of the house, balustraded on one side, with a view over parkland and the pastoral water-meadows of the river Welland. Across the north side of the site extended a Victorian conservatory or winter-garden, and at right angles to it a ballroom. Where the house once stood was now, incongruously, a wooden gardener's shed, all alone in the middle of the old foundations. Its door opened to frame a bizarre composition: a dart-board on one wall, a framed print of the Last Supper on the other, a chair and table, three feet of scorched Grinling Gibbons carving, and several used condoms on the floor. No doubt it was a local trysting-place.

Musing, I left and stealthily forced open the conservatory door to emerge into a cast-iron-canopied wonderland, and the detritus of sudden catastrophe: smashed and burnt glass, a half-burnt Regency side table, broken gilt picture frames, bits of

68. Uffington House, Lincolnshire,
south terrace, February 1980

69. Uffington House, Lincolnshire,
the ballroom, February 1980

marble, plaster fragments, a shattered gilt Georgian torchère. This brought me up sharp: this was 1958, not 1904. I stood silent and thoughtful, then pushed through the Ritz Hotel-style mirrored door that beckoned me into the ballroom.

My eyes, penetrating the gloom, travelled up a mountainous wall of hay bales to a richly gilt coved ceiling. It was not this that amazed me, however, but rather what the passageway about four feet wide around the sides of the hay contained. Take the contents of a high-quality antique shop, scoop them up and dump them roughly into this ballroom – that was the effect, and it seemed extraordinary that even a farmer should have just pushed all this into a pile without any examination, or awareness of what might be there. Imagine a Hepplewhite chair, just smashed to pieces; the top of a nineteenth-century Boulle table; at the rear, a grand piano up-ended, and a really fine neo-classical side table in a Stuart or Chambers style; masses of broken Meissen or Sèvres porcelain all over the floor; and, memorably, a Venetian glass mirror. But then, as James Lees-Milne might comment, in those days the 'lower orders' knew their place: 'Theirs not to query why.'

It seemed incredible that half a century and two world wars had not disturbed what a family left behind *in extremis*. I examined a pair of eighteenth-century duelling pistols in an ornamented leather case; a huge Renaissance bronze door knocker; and a small walnut cabinet that opened, breath-takingly, to reveal trays of gold and silver Roman coins, each one set in a labelled recess. I remember just staring at this, and the wicked thoughts rushing through my mind can be imagined. Should I fill my pockets with gold? It was spooky. Yet what was more compelling even than the coins was a large brown paper parcel labelled by the Royal Commission on Historical Manuscripts and containing the Lindsey manuscripts and letters: it had been posted back to Uffington after listing, but never opened. Among a litter of papers and letters I found the building accounts of Samuel Gray for the Victorian additions of *c.* 1845, and these I felt little compunction about 'rescuing'.

I gazed again at the coins and the bronze, abandoned the mischievous thoughts they excited, then looked down. On the floor was an Egyptian scarab. I picked it up and put it in my pocket. I have it still. Passing the shed I speculated briefly on the nubile pleasures of rural pursuits, then left as furtively as I had arrived. A few weeks later I gave the Gray accounts to the RIBA.

The discovery of Uffington haunted me. I subsequently wrote to Lady Muriel, who had inherited Uffington as the only daughter of the 12th Earl of Lindsey, commenting on what remained in the ruins. She replied that she had never been there, and that the estate was in the care of a manager. By the 1980s it had all been tidied up, the conservatory removed elsewhere, and what was left converted to a house. This was followed soon after by an application for Listed Building consent to turn the lovely park into a golf course. It was rejected out of hand.

31

Mars bars were only made from 1932

Willoughby Hall, Lincolnshire

IN 1959 I described Willoughby Hall near Ancaster, Lincolnshire, as 'a tall, gaunt, French-style house of 1873, said to be by Watkins and in ruins'; in 1989 my text was revised to read, 'Of the French-style house of 1873 by William Watkins only the stable block of 1876, with shaped gables, remains.' Today I would further revise my stylistic judgement: I believe Willoughby was a very clever adaptation from local seventeenth-century Northamptonshire and south Lincolnshire models, and that it had also benefited from the Flemish taste of Frederick Allix's wife Sophia. At the time he was working at Willoughby, Watkins had already built in 1867 the Town Hall at nearby Grantham.

I had come to Willoughby in the late afternoon from Caythorpe, its walled park and funerary monuments so redolent of the Hussey tenure. Being Lincolnshire, this was RAF country, the domain of 'Bomber' Harris. My index card said 'Mucked up by the RAF – from Cranwell', but the army were

70. Willoughby Hall, Lincolnshire,
from the north-east, April 1963

71. Willoughby Hall, Lincolnshire, vestibule, April 1963

billeted here too. I was puzzled by large numbers at least two feet high painted on the roof and thought of demolition, but learned later that the RAF used the numbers to practise precision bombing in their Mosquitoes. Even from a distance, a spookiness seemed to emanate from the ruin as I approached, a feeling not unlike that which I'd experienced at Bulwell in Nottinghamshire. I knew nothing then of Charles Hitchcock, a lunatic who, cared for by his brother the Reverend Harry, was incarcerated here from 1912 until his death in 1928. It is said that he would appear with a handkerchief on his head, and run away when approached. Another tale is attested to by old Mr Simkins, the Hitchcocks' gardener. He reported that Charley had the run of the attic floor, and was allowed out into the garden at three o'clock each afternoon, superintended by a maid. Simkins could point to the gabled window on the garden front from which Charley would sing to and stare at the moon – it seems that he would get into a frightful state if there was no moon on a night when he needed its consolation. One such night, he ran up and down the stairs so many times that he finally collapsed exhausted at the bottom. Simkins also claimed that Charley had a passion for Mars bars, which his brother used to supply in bulk. This surprised me, and later enquiries made to the Mars bars people in Slough revealed that the bars had only been marketed from 1932. Maybe Charley's ghost consumed them? The house was untenanted after Charley's death in 1928. When the army moved in, a carved French chimney-piece was there one day and gone the next, and according to Simkins, no doubt a local myth-maker, the house was badly haunted. Objects would suddenly break, as if someone had smashed them. 'A real nasty feeling the place gave,' he confessed. There were noises in the night, but it was not clear if these were the gasps of soldiers in the embrace of WRACS, or Charley's ghost moaning at the moon.

Looking back, I don't believe I have never found a ruin so unpleasant. The back parts had been used as pigsties, and stank from the inevitable muck-heap. In the stables the walls were plastered with army notices. Each stall had housed not horses but soldiers, eating around a table, and the columnar divisions had all been broken up for firewood, as had the balusters of the upper main staircase and the panelling in the dining room. Upstairs, only accessible by sidling along a wall beam over a precipitous drop, the wet rot bulged out of walls like balloons, and the stench of decay was choking. I'm sure Charley had been harmless, but he left a legacy of evil emanations. I felt cold, on this warm summer's evening.

The mode of Willoughby's demise was not uncommon: on 4 November 1964 the ruin was spectacularly blown up by 320 charges of dynamite, evoking a smug smile from its farming owner, and hurrahs from the assembled public and local reporters.

32

Ostlers, and Bertie Wild Men

Revesby Abbey, Rauceby Hall and Eresby, Lincolnshire

INCOLNSHIRE IN 1959 was still an agrarian county fixed in a time warp, despite Billy Butlin's holiday camp at Skegness and the steel mills of Scunthorpe. As late as 1900, Danish words were understood in remoter Fen villages such as Algarkirk, legacy of the centuries of mercantile links between Boston and Scandinavia. One summer's afternoon saw me clambering through rooms rampant with dry rot at Revesby Abbey. I was then sorting the William Burn–MacVicar Anderson drawings in the RIBA, and had planned to inspect their work at Rauceby, Stoke Rochford and Revesby. This last had been Sir Joseph Banks's family seat. How one wished his so-called Tahitian huts had survived. Gone also was his evocative seventeenth-century mansion, replaced by a house built in 1844 for J. Banks Stanhope, which I thought looked inviting at the end of a long vista from a grand ironwork screen and gates off the village street. Integral to the picture was the estate village, with school and almshouses laid out in the 1850s and

1860s, and C.H. Fowler's church of 1889. An airborne division and the Somerset Light Infantry had left Revesby in a frightful mess: timber joists exposed through ceilings, every chimney-piece defaced, smashed Rococo Revival furniture lying about, a room in the rear moving with dry rot, and one room with the plaster from its collapsed ceiling intermingled with books. Upstairs, Burn had created a panelled wall system with genuine German rococo woodwork alternating with his plaster panels; in a chimney-piece he had incorporated some Bavarian rococo carvings. The Continental theme had been continued into the garden with Dutch and German statuary, including a wonderful Venus with that characteristic Bavarian *contraposto*. All this statuary was later rumoured to have gone for a song to a Kings Lynn garage owner.

After Revesby I stopped at Rauceby Hall, as perfect an Early Victorian house as one could get, built for A. Peacock Willson in 1842. It stood dream-like in its lush park, and its pretty owner was cutting the hay. She gave me tea and I commiserated with her on the recent loss of her husband in a motoring accident. I admired the family paintings, all of an uncommonly interesting, Continental, Louis XIV sort. After a long pause in my peregrinations which ended in me declining to become the new master of this house, I eventually moved on, to lie for an hour on the grassy mounds of Old Bolingbroke Castle and dream of the birth of Henry IV here, in 1367. Although a signpost beckoned me to the delights of 'Mavis and Bag Enderby', I declined that offer too, and late in the afternoon came to Spilsby.

This pleasing old market town acts as a gateway to the secretive Wolds to the north. It marks, too, a change of elevation, unexpected to a traveller leaving the flat Fens where vast distances shimmer in that watery light. I needed a bed for the

72. Revesby Abbey, Lincolnshire, from the garden

73. Eresby, Lincolnshire,
the gate pier to the first court, 1959

night, and an old inn, the White Hart, looked inviting. I had already visited Belleau, that magical place lost in the Wolds where the medieval Lords Willoughby first lived and where, built into the side of a barn there, could still be found the mighty bearded head of a Wild Man or Wodewose: Wild Men were the heraldic supporters of the family coat-of-arms.

The imagination can play tricks with memory, but even now I recollect an uncanny feeling upon entering the door of the inn. The interior was a study in patinated browns: ceilings once white were dung-colour from a century of nicotine, all the woodwork was painted either drab Victorian brown or in that characteristic varnished and stippled light brown. The stone floors had been painted black, but were worn by sweeping and washing, and there was sawdust on the wooden floor of the bar. As I later discovered, it was on a par with the old Assembly Room of the White Hart at Folkingham, then likewise covered in smoky brown varnish, and smoky too the sporting pictures hanging on the walls.

At first the bar was empty, but soon the innkeeper came through a door. He wore a brown serge suit, and I remember him facially for a large protuberant hairy black mole on his cheek. My enquiry for a bed was met with surprise, as if such a request was rarely made. 'I'll call Jim,' he said, and shouted through a serving hatch. Jim was a real 'ostler', or groom, with a nut-brown face to match the White Hart's interior, dressed in a long greasy-black close-fitting coat and wearing heavy black strapped boots. He nodded and grunted, and led me up a brown panelled staircase and through a dark passage hung with that popular set of four faded prints of Sport in Black Park by Henry Alken. The bedroom was also a symphony in brown, and almost Shaker in its simplicity: just a bed, a Windsor chair, two coat-hooks on the wall, and a yellow-ochrey wash-stand,

with bowl and jug in a bright mauve flowered design. Jim
said he would bring hot water, returned with a tall copper
container, filled the jug, and left announcing that dinner was
at six – early, but the usual hour in the rural parts of the
county.

The table had been specially laid: white cloth, linen napkins,
and heavy old-fashioned 'silver' cutlery. A broth soup was followed by lamb chops, roast potatoes and greens, then rice
pudding. I was obviously being treated as something rare and
special. It pleased me. I was suffused with comfort. After dinner I took a walk through the town, then went back to write
up the day's travel notes. I remember being surprised that
there was no one in the bar. I said goodnight, and went up to
my room.

To my astonishment, I found a fire lit in the grate. A knock
at the door was Jim, carrying an old-fashioned copper bed-
warmer full of hot coals. I goggled and pinched myself. Was
this 1959, or 1859? Hardly had I laid my head on the pillow
than I fell asleep, a heavy drugged sort of sleep, of a kind I
experienced only once again, after a massage in a Japanese tea
house in Kyoto. I suddenly awoke to a knock: it was morning,
and there was Jim with hot water. I packed my knapsack and
found a scrumptious breakfast awaiting me, of the sort I still
laughingly refer to as 'The best of British Rail', more recently
as 'Snake's Comfort'. The table was again immaculately laid,
and the surprise that made me pinch myself yet again was a
neatly ironed and folded newspaper.

Years later I wondered if it had all been a dream, and I
remember sitting at the table at the time, distracted by the
uncanniness of everything. But it was time to leave, to mount
not a horse, as would have befitted service by a real ostler, but
my Lambretta. I was anxious to see the Bertie and d'Eresby

74. Spilsby, Lincolnshire, St James's church:
a Bertie Wild Man *c.* 1580s, supporting the Bertie arms

family chapel inside Spilsby church, and to discover the site of Eresby, the long-demolished seat of the Berties nearby. In the chapel, in front of the spectacular tomb to Richard Bertie and Baroness Willoughby de Eresby of the 1580s, I stared at the supporting figures, two Wild Men, and for some reason, laughing out loud, made an idiotic remark such as 'You don't frighten me, Wild Men', and stamped symbolically on their slab.

From the church, a great avenue marches south to the site of old Eresby, sadly now bisected by the Spilsby Bypass. Eresby is a poignant place, marked by a monumental single gate pier with a huge urn, late seventeenth-century and not unlike similar gates at the Bertie house at Uffington or at Burley-on-the-Hill. The medieval house onto which Lord Willoughby 'intendeth to build sumptuously' in the 1560s, according to Leland, was burnt in 1769. Beyond the gate pier I found the outline of the first court, an Artisan Mannerist brick stable, and a fascinating configuration in turf outline of all the formal gardens – sunken parterres, terraces and canals – made by Stephen Switzer for the 1st Duke of Ancaster, who about 1710 may have contemplated a new large house here by Sir John Vanbrugh. Garden archaeology would be enriched, I thought, if this lost garden were excavated.

I turned again towards the church, and about half-way down the avenue the Wild Men expressed their disapproval of my lack of respect, inflicting a sudden convulsing back pain that caused me to collapse onto the grass. My head nearly touched my knees, and I was cemented in this position. I could only cry 'Help! Help!', my alarm increasing as no one came my way. As my cries became more strident, a little girl with a barking dog arrived. She took one look, shrieked but uttered no word, and ran back along the avenue crying. Ten minutes later a farmer arrived, but could not move me, and left to call an ambulance. Half an hour later, two ambulance men brought a stretcher and, like so many dead Berties and d'Eresbys, I was carried down the avenue, as if on a bier to a last resting place in the chapel.

Even on the X-ray table in Lincoln I remained doubled up. Perplexed, the doctors put me to bed. I won't even try to describe the operations with the bottle, and later with the pan. Doctors and student interns came to stare at me as I remained in this contorted position for three days. Suddenly, on the fourth dawn I awoke to a relaxation of the muscles. The doctors laughed at my diagnosis of Wild Men's Revenge, but I knew better. Ever since, I have been humbly respectful whenever I think of Berties and d'Eresbys visiting that great Lincolnshire castle of Grimsthorpe – and I sincerely hope that the Wild Men wreaked their revenge on the Ministry of Transport officials responsible for the Spilsby Bypass.

33

Of pet lions, Coade peacocks, and Vyner ghosts

Haverholme Priory, Bloxholm Hall, Blankney House, Nocton Hall, Tupholme Hall and Gautby Great Park, Lincolnshire

THE SPRING OF 1959 found me in Sleaford to make a tour of houses in distress. I had read of Haverholme Priory and of the 12th Earl of Winchilsea's pet lion, which visitors were apt to find unrestrainedly reclining on the sofa. Lord Winchilsea's other eccentricity was to amass one of the largest-known collections of eagles' eggs. My notes indicated a Gothick house done up for Sir Jenison William Gordon in 1788, then grandiosely rebuilt in Tudor style by H.E. Kendall in 1830. At his death in 1831 Gordon left the estate to the Earl of Winchilsea of the day in trust for Murray Edward Gordon Finch-Hatton, who succeeded as the 12th Earl in 1887. As with the Winchilseas' Eastwell in Kent, Haverholme was a casualty of the First World War, advertised for sale in 1921 and demolished in 1927. But something remained, I was assured.

I found the huge park bounded by the river Slea and bisected by a lane from Ewerby. As I turned off the main road, a handsome stone bridge with ample balls and a 1893 date-

75. Haverholme Priory, Lincolnshire,
remaining centre of the house

76. Bloxholme Hall, Lincolnshire, gate to the church

77. Bloxholme Hall, Lincolnshire, Peacock entrance front

stone gave a misleading hint of estate care, for turning the corner by some farm buildings I found the usual sordid stable range and scatter of rubbish. The Kendall entrance tower stood tall and jagged, like a broken tooth, in its ruin in the centre of the old foundations of the house. I leaned on a crumbling balustrade to look across the ploughed park. Wilfrid Scawen Blunt's description of the house was 'melancholy always', Blunt having stayed here with Denys Finch-Hatton of *Out of Africa* fame.

Distracted by a reference on the map to a Seltzer Spring nearby I neglected to divert to the site of the Gilbertine Catley Abbey, but instead took the rural B1188 for the next ruined house, at Bloxholm. Rupert Gunnis had extolled this place, commenting on the great Coade-stone peacock that had toppled from its central gable, crashing to the ground. Bloxholm presented a scene typical of this flat, fenny landscape: the ruined house huddled with the church in arboreal seclusion, a green island in the surrounding flatlands. Nearby was the estate hamlet, and further away the long approach drive, announced by Peacock Lodge. I noticed General Manners' coat-of-arms dated 1812 in Coade-stone over the church porch. The house stood there, a tall ruin silhouetted against the sky. It was impossible to negotiate the rooms because of the danger of falling through the floors. A tree was growing up through the hall. Bloxholm was a striking example of that Cromwellian style known as Artisan Mannerism, reputedly built by Ciprian Thornton in the 1660s or 1670s, given a new canted front in 1772 for Lord Robert Manners, who topped it with the famous peacock, and then extended by Vulliamy with stables in 1825 and wings in 1827. I left thinking that the Venetian window in the earlier south front, which was so near collapse as to seem to sway in the wind, was 'highly uncommon' for its date.

78. Blankney Hall, Lincolnshire, entrance front, 1961

I consulted the map: next stop Blankney Park, with a glance *en route* at Ashby Hall in Ashby de la Launde, but missing out Vulliamy's gothic stables. The architectural history of Blankney, long the seat of the Chaplins, and after 1896 of the Earl of Londesborough, is unsupported by documents. Before his attainder in 1715 the Jacobite Lord Widdrington may have employed Stephen Switzer for planting, but the Chaplins bought the estate in 1719 and what I had before me was the Palladian house built by a later Thomas Chaplin. The contrast between the lushness of the picturesque Early Victorian estate village of the 1830s and 1840s that enfolds the place and the pathetic decay of the house that once gave it meaning was very telling.

Blankney was first vandalised by RAF and USAF requisition, then burnt out in 1945. Nevertheless, the skeletal structure of the interior was still there, and I was able to negotiate between the remains of fine Palladian ceilings, hanging down in huge pendulous lumps, rain cascading from top to bottom. There were remains of rich late Victorian Crace-style decoration for Henry Chaplin (1840–1923), who local history claims was ruined by his lavish way of living, his passion for the horse and hunting, and the expensive care he bestowed on the estate, including rebuilding the church (by Carpenter) in 1878. As I left I looked up at the bust of Galba above the pediment of the door and wondered what its fate would be.

In the eighteenth century this part of the county was a 'blasted heath', the haunt of highwaymen, so on my way to Nocton I made a short diversion to see what remained of the Dunston Pillar, built by Sir Francis Dashwood in 1751 as a beacon for travellers. In 1810 the lanthorn was replaced by Mrs Coade's statue of George III, and poor John Willson, the mason fixing it, fell off the top. He is buried in Harmston churchyard with the epitaph 'He who erected the noble King/Is here now laid by Death's sharp sting'. I believe the RAF removed 'the noble King' as he was a danger to aircraft.

I knew that at Nocton I would find the 1st Earl of Ripon's Tudoresque house of 1841 in an estate village not unlike Blankney's, with picturesque cottages. Dominating all was Scott's All Saints of 1860. What really drew me there on this day of decay and ruin was my curiosity to know whether anything remained of the huge Jacobean house built for the Ellys family, particularly Sir William Ellys, in the 1670s. Alas! his magical house was completely gone, but fate determined that I should find, hidden away in shrubberies, the poignant remains of one of his garden pavilions in brick and stone, with consoled *oeil-de-boeuf* openings, bolection windows and door.

I had one other house to visit, and it was late afternoon. I would have to postpone seeing George Basevi's derelict Longhills of 1838 at Branston, but must take the road across

79. Tupholme Hall, Lincolnshire, entrance front

80. Gautby Great Park, Lincolnshire, the offices

Nocton Fen, cross the river Witham at Bardney and seek out Tupholme Hall, probably built by Thomas Vyner before he died in 1710. The ruins of Tupholme Abbey delayed me briefly, for their remoteness, but Tupholme's enticing tall brick silhouette could be seen at the edge of a wood to the north. I was captivated here as much by the fenland silence as by this Williamite doll's house with its Artisan Mannerist pavilions, sitting empty as if awaiting a lover who sadly would never come, the garden and park ploughed right up to the walls. Empty it remained, until it was outrageously demolished by Rank Pensions Ltd in 1984, despite concerted protest. On this day in 1959 I found its simple interior decayed but otherwise as perfect as when it was first built, with panelling, mouldings and a fine oak balustered stair.

It was early evening, and the comfortable White Hart at Lincoln sang its siren song, but how could I ignore the site of the Vyners' Great House at Gautby Great Park only a few miles away? Robert Vyner had bought the estate, an ancient park even then, in the early eighteenth century. Abandoned and demolished as early as 1874, a casualty of the Agricultural Depression, few places have such an air of deserted splendour. I found an early eighteenth-century brick Artisan stable, and the remains of the long canal – but I wondered whether the sculptor Jaspar Latham's equestrian statue of Charles II could really have stood on an island here when it was moved from London to Gautby in 1779 (it is now at Newby Hall in Yorkshire). Dusk was closing in fast as I entered the lonely church built for the Vyners in 1754. Peering through the gloom, I could barely discern the Vyner tombs. All of a sudden, a huge black cat shot out of a corner, and out the door: the Vyner phantom expelled. The White Hart called again, now irresistibly.

34

'They've come to read the meter, Mum'

Narford Hall, Norfolk

A T FIRST THIS is not my story, but belongs to Francis Watson, at a time when he was Deputy Keeper of The Wallace Collection in 1955. His study of Venetian painters in England demanded a visit to Narford Hall in Norfolk to see Antonio Pellegrini's Painted Hall. More than it was famous for Pellegrini, Narford was notorious in the county for Mrs Fountaine's rebuff of Queen Mary at the door when Her Majesty came over from nearby Houghton on a scavenging visit. Narford was always bracketed with Calke Abbey and Shirburn Castle as one of the more tantalisingly inaccessible houses in England. Architectural historians vied with one another to be able to say they had been to Narford, so even Francis was not hopeful of success. Imagine his astonishment, therefore, to receive a letter from Mrs Fountaine inviting him for the weekend. Fearful of his wife Jane's famous habit of speaking before thinking, he left her at home with the cats. No doubt he was still reeling from a recent weekend at Windsor, when Queen

Elizabeth asked how he liked the Boulle commode in the Grand Corridor. As he was complimenting Her Majesty on her judgement, Jane interrupted in her usual loud, shrill voice: 'But that's not what you told me, Francis. You said she was a silly old thing to put a commode in the sunlight there!' So Jane was left at home.

Mrs Fountaine's first words after greeting Francis were, 'And remember – no photographs, Mr Watson.' 'That won't stop me,' thought Francis. 'I'll get up very early in the morning.' Exulting in the thrill of being in this house denied to almost everyone, Francis studied the Pellegrini canvases in the hall, aware of the tradition that they had been discarded from Burlington House and given by Lord Burlington to his friend and mentor, the famous collector Sir Andrew Fountaine. Of course, Francis had no way of knowing that later cleaning of the canvases for a subsequent owner, Commander Andrew Fountaine, would reveal that they had indeed been cut to fit the existing hall. The paintings simply had to be photographed, and Francis devised plans for 4.30 the following morning.

Dawn was breaking as Francis crept down the stairs, set up his camera and flash and snapped away. His feeling of triumph was short-lived, however. As he was about to creep silently back upstairs, all of a sudden a hall door opened and there stood Mrs Fountaine, in her night-dress. Without a word she snatched his camera, efficiently exposed the film, and left the way she had come with the command, 'You may leave now, Mr Watson.' He returned forlornly to Jane and the cats.

During the late 1950s I must have written to Mrs Fountaine at least four times in increasingly desperate efforts to gain access to this house. In 1960 Mark Girouard and his father

81. Narford Hall, Norfolk, entrance front

Dickie suggested I try again, and this time it worked: a post-card arrived saying simply 'Saturday 11.00 am. Mrs Fountaine' – nothing more. Although it was not specified, we guessed she meant the coming Saturday. We three stayed in nearby King's Lynn, and that morning approached with mounting excite-ment, almost drooling, bubbling with comments: 'Look, there's Henry Bell's 1702 front', and 'That must be the Library wing', knowing that Sir Andrew Fountaine had been its ama-teur architect. We were dismayed by the dull rebuilding *c.* 1866 by R. Ketton of Norwich that had preserved Bell's south entrance front but externally swallowed up nearly every-thing else. So we were on an architectural 'high'. We knocked at the door, and waited – and waited, and waited. It seemed an age. We knocked again, and waited even longer. Then I did a circuit of the house, hoping to see a face at a window, but returned to knock and wait yet again. We despaired. We talked of giving up. But suddenly, a lock turned, a maid's face appeared: 'What do you want here?' To which we answered, 'Mrs Fountaine asked us to see the house today,' and gave her the postcard. The door shut abruptly, and yet again we had to wait and wait.

Once more the sound of the lock, the appearance of the face, but now 'Come in.' We entered a vestibule and turned into the hall which held the glory of Venice condensed into one room. However, it was not Pellegrini's work that held us transfixed – it was the stuffed ostrich standing in the middle of the room – and it moved! It was Mrs Fountaine, in an ostrich-feather dress and an ostrich-feather hat that covered her face. A voice from behind the feathers exclaimed, 'I've lost my glasses and can't see. Who are you, how many?'

We talk, and she warms to us; we gaze dreamily at the paintings, aware that Minerva and Arachne cannot be seen because the large side table in front of them is piled to the ceiling with what appear to be (mostly unopened) copies of *The Times*, the later ones just thrown up to the top of the heap. Mrs Fountaine talks engagingly and, to our surprise, most intelligently about the history of the house and its contents. She knows about Bell as a gentleman architect, of her ancestor Sir Andrew, and of Andien de Clermont the ceiling painter who worked here about 1735 when Sir Andrew's friend, Henry Herbert, 9th Earl of Pembroke, was advising on interior decoration with his amanuensis Roger Morris. Then we hear a distant knock at the door.

'I am not expecting anyone,' said Mrs Fountaine, 'and I had forgotten about you.' The maid returned to report. 'A man and woman with a clipboard, Mum. Maybe from the Council, perhaps to read the meter.' 'You'd better see them,' said Mrs Fountaine. 'I didn't think they worked on Saturdays.' There is a ripple of amusement on our part when the maid announces 'A Dr and Mrs Pevsner asking to see the house. From the Buildings Council.' We laugh hysterically, and assure Mrs Fountaine that this is a coincidence, not a conspiracy. So in come Nikolaus and Lola, she indeed with a clipboard in her hand. They are as confused as Mrs Fountaine, and can't see the funny side of the situation. We wondered whether there could be anything more off-putting to the landed classes than to arrive at the front door looking as though you'd come to read the meter.

Fortunately Mrs Fountaine took it all in her stride, and we toured the house, marvelling at the beautiful Venetian library but hurried out of it immediately I spied a copy of Lord Burlington's *Fabbriche Antiche* and asked to see it. We gazed with sadness at the Pembroke–Morris octagonal china closet and cabinet that once displayed Sir Andrew's great collection of maiolica and Limoges enamels, sold in 1884. We marvelled at Clermont's ceilings in the Antique style. As we left, with ample notes from Mrs Fountaine's conversation, we reckoned that never had we been in a house so redolent of its collector–owner. We waved to Nikolaus and Lola sitting in their car with their clipboard. When Nikolaus's *Norfolk* came out in 1962, I saw that he had managed to get most of the facts wrong. So much for clipboards.

35

Le Brun and the Escalier des Ambassadeurs, Versailles

Staunton Hall, Nottinghamshire

W<small>E STAYED WITH</small> Henry Thorold at Marston Hall, Lincolnshire in 1960 with the prospect of visiting Staunton Hall, Nottinghamshire, just across the county border. Henry filled in a little of the history of the Hall. The fame of the squarson there, Henry Staunton, apparently rested upon his great tome, *The Stauntons of Staunton*, which I have been unable to trace. Eileen shivered when Henry warned us to wrap up warmly because Staunton church was cold: Marston was her first English country-house-weekend experience, and Marston itself was cold enough. We were to attend the Harvest Festival service, then dine with Henry Staunton in the Hall.

My only memory of that festival was of two squarsons delivering secular homilies – and tedious they were – on the longevity of family possession. Yes, the church *was* bitterly cold. What a relief to leave that archaic ritual for the sanctuary of Staunton Hall. Again my memory is imprecise, but the

82. Staunton Hall, Nottinghamshire, entrance front

general impression I retain of the interior is of smoke-stained ceilings, dark unrestored wood or paintwork, and hundreds of very bad and very dirty provincial portraits, hung in rows, mostly by face-painters from Nottingham. One face looked like any other, and they all looked like Henry Staunton.

Dinner was a delight. First the ubiquitous sherry, generally to be avoided unless known to be of exceptional quality, then to dinner in the hall – certainly a hall-like room, with a long oak table in the centre. There was one oddity: a cleared space about a foot wide extended the whole length of the table, and the candle-stands were set between the diners and just in from the edge of the table. The reason for the space became apparent after the soup. The main course arrived, carried in ceremonially by two maids: a large cut of beef reposing upon a silver trolley on wheels. This was set at one end, where Henry Staunton began the proceedings by cutting off his slices of beef; then the cart was pulled along the length of the table, left–right–left–right, each diner attending to his or her portion.

Potatoes and vegetables followed – all pushed along the centre.

Coffee followed in a drawing room of white-painted, cream-curtained Edwardian decor; and Edwardian too the furniture, maybe Louis Quinzey. My eyes lighted upon a portfolio stand. I itched to trawl through it, and was emboldened to do so. A few county maps, some sporting prints, various pretty flower prints – and then my hands shook a little and my heart gave an extra thump as I pulled out a fine large red chalk drawing of one corner of a very grand baroque ceiling. It looked to be French, and seventeenth-century, and the subject was faintly familiar.

It was so out-of-place in a house whose squires seemed unlikely ever to have strayed beyond their Nottinghamshire acres. The pictures on the walls bespoke a family to whom anything Continental was alien. 'What is this?' I asked Henry Thorold. As he didn't know, he suggested I take it back with me to London – and with Henry Staunton's blessing I did. The identification of the subject proved easy – it was no less than a design for Charles le Brun's *Escalier des Ambassadeurs* at Versailles, a vigorous composition, probably one of the drawings prepared in Le Brun's office for the standard set of engravings.

Now what should I do? I lusted for it, to add to my Laguerres, Thornhills, Riccis and Amigonis, but how could I acquire it at reasonable cost and without alerting Henry Staunton to the fact that it was a treasure? Henry Thorold suggested I should simply write and ask him to put a price on it: 'He'll ask you for a valuation.' I did, but he didn't! I have his letter somewhere still: 'My Harvest Festival church account is nine pounds five shillings and six pence in arrears,' wrote the squarson of Staunton. I sent him ten pounds, and gleefully took Le Brun to the framers.

Epilogue

The period I look back on seems far-distant now. For me it was one of uncertainty, as it was for the houses I discovered. No motorways existed, and trains puffed along branch lines at a leisurely pace. Main roads were still safe for cyclists, cars were banned from Youth Hostels, and motorists were kind to hitch-hikers. England was a very different place from what it is today. There was time to stand and stare – and for me that meant time, too, for fishing. In retrospect, I believe I sensed an affinity with those houses that stood awaiting their sentence. I saw myself as their Apostle.

There were others who sensed the tragedy of those losses, not least my friends Jim Lees-Milne and Derek Sherborn, Howard Colvin and Rupert Gunnis. Yet the demolitions seemed unstoppable. The amenity societies were too genteel, their concerns too selective. The Georgian Group of today would never meekly acquiesce in the demolition of Wilton Park, as it did in 1962. I can recall few protests from the regions. There was no rallying cry such as was later voiced by SAVE Britain's Heritage. Confronted by those legions of lost houses, so many of pre-eminent quality (many who visited it will remember my mournful voice tolling out the endless list of names at the 'Destruction' exhibition), it seems impossible to single out one to encapsulate the whole fateful period of the 1950s and 1960s. Nevertheless, Burwell's destruction continued to haunt me long after the tragic event, and still does.

Although this has been a text of despair, there were a few early flickerings of hope. Soon after the war, some young owners or heirs rallied to save their houses by opening them to the public. The Duke of Bedford at Woburn, or Lord Brooke at Warwick, were pioneers in the 'stately home business', which has now burgeoned to such an extent that there is an Historic Houses Association to protect the interests of country house owners. The National Trust was a lifeline, and has saved more country houses than any other organisation in the world. If any event can be singled out as representing a turning-point or watershed, it was surely the 'Destruction of the Country House' exhibition in 1974, organised by Marcus Binney and myself. Not only did it express the loss in dramatic and theatrical terms, but it offered owners hope instead of despair. It displayed the growing mettle of the Historic Buildings Council in offering grant aid. It demonstrated the viability of converting large houses (such as Shardeloes, for example) into flats, as pioneered by Mutual Households. It showed the many advantages for organisations in urban centres of relocating to rural situations, and with today's electronic technology this is an even more attractive option. Of course, not least, the 'Destruction' exhibition was the catalyst for Marcus Binney to found SAVE Britain's Heritage as a powerful campaigning organ. After twenty years of protest, SAVE has done more than any other heritage organisation to still the voices of despair and lament.

In the fifty years since my country-house odyssey started with that visit to the Langley Park auction in 1946, 31 of the 53 houses I mention here have been demolished. Of the rest, Bulstrode, Dogmersfield, Langley, Nocton, Rauceby and Slindon are in religious or secular institutional use. Shardeloes has been converted into flats. Bridgefoot, Hungershall, Iver Grove, Narford, Oving, Staunton, Wulf Hall and Wrotham are still private houses. Erddig belongs to the National Trust, Kenwood to English Heritage, and Lydiard Tregoze to Swindon Borough Council. Highcliffe is being restored by Christchurch Borough Council with the aid of public funds, and Painshill is under exemplary restoration by the Painshill Park Trust. Shurland is still a tragic ruin, and Ingress, Revesby and Breakspears stand empty, their future uncertain. No one could claim that every one of the 31 lost houses should have been saved, but each of them possessed some interior detail worthy of note, and as I walked their empty rooms it was always in the consciousness that they were once a stage for the lives of their occupants, as will be obvious from my text. Nevertheless, if we were presented with the same situation today I am certain that Richings, Badger, Draycot Cerne, Belvedere, Winchendon, Stratton, Fairford, Scrivelsby, Bure Homage, Willingham, Bayons, Watnall, Burwell, Panton, Bloxholm, Blankney and Tupholme would be fought for and saved. I think Onslow, Kempshott, West Willoughby and Haverholme might still have been lost, but even the unalluring Bulwell would surely have survived to find some use in the urban environs of Nottingham. It is quite extraordinary that the future of the country house is probably brighter now than at any other time in this century. Ours is no longer a land in which demolition men arrive every few days in their tumbrils with sledge-hammer, picks and ball-and-chain to execute their victims.

Indebtedness

M Y RECOLLECTIONS OF houses seen more than forty years ago have naturally blurred, despite notes. Surfing my memory, the houses themselves and events associated with them are clear, their parks and gardens less so. A corrective was the National Monuments Record at Swindon, and I have only praise for the kindliness of the staff there, even if I must confess that what I found in the photo image was not always what I had disinterred from my memory. It was sometimes necessary to relive past encounters by topographical forays, either with my son Lucian as an agreeable chauffeur, or with Tim Knox, Todd Longstaffe Gowan and my wife Eileen. A problem that has never been solved is exactly who occupied these houses during the Second World War – and no wonder, if Rolls Park in Essex saw a succession of eighteen regiments in just four years. I have received great help in this from the archivists and staff of county record offices and from local history librarians in county and town libraries; the incumbents of relevant churches have also been helpful. I have a few special acknowledgements to make, to the following: Bruce Bailey, for photographs of Rupert Gunnis's house; Audrey Baker, for help on Bulstrode; Sir Howard Colvin, for information and photographs; Ron Honey, Langley and Black Park estate manager, for his extraordinary local knowledge; Andrew Langton, the Waddesden Estate Agent, and Edward Sandland for photographs of the Winchendon pavilion; Peter Reid, for his compendious photographic knowledge and archive; Dr Stella Rowlands, the historian of Iver, for her generosity in sharing her knowledge of local houses; my old friend and travelling companion Derek Sherborn, for reliving houses we visited together; Tim Knox, for reading and improving my texts; and Eileen, for her hovering presence. Finally, and certainly not least, I have benefited from John Murray, as a wise and most agreeable publisher, and his most excellent editor Liz Robinson.

Index

Page numbers in *italic* refer to the illustrations

233